True Crimes Trivia and Activity Book

All rights are reserved 2024 by Life Style Daily. No part of this publication may be reproduced, stored in a retrieval system or transmitted in any form or by any means, electronic, mechanical, photocopying, recording or otherwise, without prior permission.

Table of contents

1. Introduction to Forensics 3
2. The History of True Crime 6
3. Famous Criminal Cases 12
4. Crime Puzzles and Quizzes 21
5. Criminal Profiling 41
6. Crime Scene Investigation 47
7. Famous Detectives and Investigations 55
8. Notorious Trials: The Case of O.J. Simpson 67
9. Life After Crime: Social and Psychological Consequences 79
10. Quiz: "Which Murderer?" 103
11. The Ultimate Test: Criminal Challenge 107
12. Solutions 117

1. Introduction to Forensics

Each of us has, at one time or another, followed a true crime story with fascination, trying to unravel the mystery of a crime or understand what drives the minds of serial killers. Forensics, the science of investigating crimes, has long captured the attention not only of detectives and experts but also of everyday people, who seek answers about human nature in these dark stories.

Why are we drawn to crime? Perhaps it's because crime mysteries allow us to step into the role of a detective. Maybe it's because exploring the motivations of criminals helps us better understand our own fears and the darker sides of reality. Or perhaps we simply enjoy the thrill that comes with solving a mystery.

In this book, we'll take you on a journey through some of the most intriguing aspects of forensics. From the famous cases of serial killers and gripping courtroom dramas to psychological analyses that help track down criminals. We've also prepared quizzes, puzzles, and brainteasers for you to test your investigative skills and knowledge of forensic science.

Get ready for an exciting journey through the world of crime and investigations. Do you have what it takes to be a detective? Let's find out!

What is Forensics?

Forensics is a multidisciplinary science that combines chemistry, biology, psychology, computer science, and law to understand how crimes are committed and how to identify those responsible. If you think it's just about collecting fingerprints and interviewing witnesses—think again!

Every crime is like a puzzle that needs to be pieced together from thousands of small details. Detectives, forensic technicians, and profilers work together to uncover the truth—from blood spatter analysis and digital evidence on victims' computers to psychological assessments of suspects.

Forensics isn't just about catching criminals; it's also an art of deduction and logic, drawing conclusions from seemingly insignificant details. As Sherlock Holmes famously said, "It's always the little details that reveal the truth."

The History and Development of Investigative Science

The roots of forensic science trace back to ancient times, though the term itself didn't exist then. Even in ancient Rome, attempts were made to solve crimes based on evidence, though the methods were, to say the least, far from today's standards. In medieval times, local judges or inquisitors often took on detective roles, and verdicts were often based more on interpretation than on concrete evidence.

The turning point came in the 19th century with the development of natural sciences and technology, which laid the foundations of modern forensics. French detective Eugène François Vidocq was among the first to introduce systematic investigations, while Alphonse Bertillon pioneered methods for identifying criminals through body measurements—a precursor to modern fingerprinting.

In the 20th century, forensic science evolved even faster, with the introduction of DNA analysis, chemical trace examination, and computer-based investigative techniques. Today, detectives have access to tools that early investigators could only dream of.

Forensics and Pop Culture: Why Are We Fascinated by Crime?

Have you ever wondered why we're so drawn to crime shows and true-crime stories? Perhaps it's natural curiosity—there's a bit of a detective in all of us that loves solving mysteries. Or maybe it's something deeper.

Crime exists at the edge of our understanding—both terrifying and fascinating. Shows like Mindhunter and True Detective draw us in with dark stories while giving us hope that justice will prevail. True crime cases, like those about Ted Bundy or the Zodiac Killer, stir emotions by showing how thin the line can be between an "ordinary" person and a murderer.

Forensics isn't just about investigations—it's a journey into the human mind, full of psychological puzzles and moral dilemmas. Perhaps that's why we're so captivated; it lets us understand a bit more about ourselves.

2. The History of True Crime

Crimes in Ancient and Medieval Times

Crime has accompanied humanity since the dawn of civilization. Though today we associate criminal activity with the modern world, brutal and shocking crimes were everyday occurrences in ancient and medieval times. The difference, however, lay in the methods of investigation, which were... let's say, far more primitive.

- Ancient Times: Crime in the Shadow of the Law

In ancient Mesopotamia, one of the earliest known legal codes, the Code of Hammurabi, set out clear punishments for various crimes. The "eye for an eye" principle was strictly enforced—crimes like theft, murder, or fraud could lead to the loss of limbs or even one's life.

In ancient Rome, crime and politics often went hand in hand. Perhaps the most famous crime of that era was the assassination of Julius Caesar in 44 BCE. The conspiracy among senators that led to Caesar's death not only shocked Rome but also marked a turning point in the history of the Empire, illustrating how political intrigue, ambition, and betrayal could result in high-profile assassinations.

- The Middle Ages: Murder as a Way of Life

Now, moving to the dark Middle Ages, where law and order were often at the mercy of local rulers, justice took on a brutal form. Public executions were a common spectacle, and criminals were pursued primarily based on rumors and accusations.

One of the most infamous figures of medieval Europe was Vlad the Impaler, known as the inspiration behind the Dracula legend. In 15th-century Wallachia, Vlad gained notoriety as a particularly ruthless ruler who ordered his enemies to be impaled. His gruesome tactics were so horrifying that they continue to inspire tales of vampires and monsters to this day.

Another example of medieval brutality was Gilles de Rais, a French knight and close ally of Joan of Arc. Though he was a war hero, he became infamous as one of Europe's first documented serial killers. Gilles was accused of torturing and murdering dozens of children, and his crimes shook France, symbolizing the moral decay and corruption within the nobility.

- Law and Punishment

In ancient and medieval times, criminal investigations looked nothing like they do today. Without scientific methods, investigations relied on witnesses, accusations, and often torture to extract "confessions." Punishments were extremely harsh, ranging from execution and torture to exile.

It wasn't until later centuries that more organized investigative systems began to develop. Nevertheless, even in ancient and medieval times, the foundations for future forensic science were being laid: crimes were examined, and efforts were made to bring perpetrators to justice, however barbaric the methods may have been.

- ## **Crime in the 19th Century: The Rise of Serial Killers**

The 19th century was a period of dynamic change—from the Industrial Revolution and scientific advancements to the birth of modern forensics. It was during this time that the first serial killers emerged, terrifying and captivating society on an unprecedented scale.

- ### London in the Shadow of Jack the Ripper

One of the most terrifying serial killers of this era was Jack the Ripper. Late 19th-century London, especially the Whitechapel district, was a place rife with poverty, crime, and prostitution. In 1888, a series of brutal murders targeting women shocked the area and remain unsolved to this day. Jack the Ripper struck with surgical precision, leading the police to suspect that the killer might have had medical knowledge.

Despite intensive police efforts and media attention, Jack the Ripper's identity was never uncovered. He became a symbol of the elusive killer, and his crimes passed into legend, inspiring countless books, films, and conspiracy theories.

- ### A Killer in Paris: Dr. Marcel Petiot

Another early example of a serial killer was Dr. Marcel Petiot. Although his crimes occurred in the early 20th century, his story has roots in 19th-century Paris, where medicine and crime were often intertwined. Petiot used his medical skills to deceive and murder his victims, especially during World War II when he promised people safe passage from occupied France only to kill them instead. His story illustrates how criminals could exploit chaos and social distrust in times of crisis.

- ### H.H. Holmes: The Murderous Architect

In the United States, the late 19th century saw the emergence of H.H. Holmes, considered one of America's first serial killers. Holmes built his infamous "Murder Castle" in Chicago—a building filled with traps, hidden corridors, and torture chambers where he murdered many victims. His targets were often people visiting Chicago for the 1893 World's Fair.

Holmes was not only a brutal murderer but also a con artist who profited from his crimes. His story highlights how the anonymity of large cities and the industrial revolution provided the perfect setting for criminals to evade justice.

- The Birth of Modern Forensics

The 19th century also marked the beginnings of organized methods for apprehending criminals. Police departments grew in strength, fingerprinting was introduced, and interest in criminal psychology increased, all contributing to a better understanding of serial killers. In 1888, French scientist Alphonse Bertillon developed a system for measuring the body dimensions of criminals, the first step toward identifying criminals through scientific methods.

The 19th century gave rise to modern forensics, and serial killers like Jack the Ripper and H.H. Holmes became symbols of evil that both fascinated and terrified society. This period opened a new era in crime investigation, where crimes ceased to be anonymous, and investigators began using science to bring criminals to justice.

20th and 21st Century Crime: From the Mafia to Cybercrime

The 20th and 21st centuries have introduced entirely new types of crime, shaped by urbanization, technological advancement, and globalization. Crime became more organized, with modern criminals operating on an international scale, using not only brute force but also sophisticated technologies and intricate networks. Here, we'll focus on two major areas of crime: the mafia and cybercrime.

- The Mafia: Rulers of the Underworld

One of the most influential criminal phenomena of the 20th century was the mafia—organized crime syndicates that became a powerful force both in Europe and the United States. Originally referring to a secret organization from 19th-century Sicily, the term "mafia" expanded in the 20th century to describe a global criminal empire.

The most infamous of these groups was Cosa Nostra, the Sicilian mafia, which controlled large parts of the economy and exerted political influence. In the American mafia scene, figures like Al Capone and Lucky Luciano were even more terrifying than their fictionalized counterparts, such as the Corleone family in The Godfather.

Al Capone, known as "Scarface," was one of the most powerful mob bosses of the 1920s and 30s, especially during Prohibition when alcohol was banned. The mafia controlled illegal alcohol distribution, reaping enormous profits. Capone dominated Chicago's underworld, but ultimately it was not murder or smuggling, but tax evasion that led to his imprisonment.

Italian mafia structures were mirrored worldwide. In Russia, mafia-linked gangs grew powerful after the fall of the Soviet Union, while in Japan, the Yakuza became synonymous with organized crime. These organizations controlled not only drug and arms trafficking but also gambling, prostitution, and extortion.

- ### Cybercrime: Crime in the Digital Age

With technological advancements, the 21st century brought about a new kind of crime—cybercrime. Rather than physical weapons, modern criminals use computers, the internet, and digital tools to target their victims remotely.

Hackers can infiltrate banking systems, steal personal data, and even destabilize entire nations. One of the most infamous examples of cybercrime was the 2017 WannaCry ransomware attack, which infected computers worldwide, blocking access to data and demanding a ransom for their release. Victims included individuals, large corporations, and government institutions.

Another notorious cybercrime was the WikiLeaks data leak and the hacking activities linked to the 2016 U.S. presidential election. These incidents demonstrated how the internet can serve as a powerful weapon in the hands of criminals, capable of influencing global politics.

- ### 21st Century Crime: A Borderless Threat

One of the most alarming aspects of contemporary crime is its global reach. While criminals once operated locally or within a single country, today both mafia organizations and cybercriminals cross national borders. The internet allows hackers to target victims worldwide, and international mafia groups control drug and arms trafficking on every continent.

In the 21st century, criminals increasingly combine traditional methods with modern technologies, challenging law enforcement to employ more advanced tools to catch them. The challenges facing contemporary law enforcement are greater than ever, with cybercrime emerging as one of the fastest-growing threats.

The Influence of Media and Technology on Forensics

Modern investigations and crimes are deeply intertwined with media and technology, which have played a major role in shaping public perceptions of crime and advancing investigative methods. In the 20th and 21st centuries, media—whether print, radio, television, or the internet—have had a profound impact on the development of forensics and on society's approach to criminal cases.

- ## Media: The Power to Shape Public Opinion

Media have always been essential in informing the public about crimes, but it wasn't until the 20th century that they became a driving force in criminal investigations. The Lindbergh case from the 1930s, involving the kidnapping and murder of the famous aviator Charles Lindbergh's son, was one of the first major cases where mass media played a key role in publicizing the crime. Newspapers covered every detail of the investigation, and the case was so widely reported that it was called the "trial of the century."

In later decades, killers like Jack the Ripper even used the media to manipulate public opinion. The infamous letters Jack sent to London newspapers, taunting the police and full of cryptic messages, contributed to his dark legend.

With the rise of television, crime reporting in the second half of the 20th century allowed the public to follow court cases and investigations more closely. In high-profile cases, such as the O.J. Simpson trial, live broadcasts drew millions of viewers and heavily influenced public perception.

- ## Technology: A Forensic Revolution

One of the most revolutionary tools in forensics has been technology. The development of computers, databases, and investigative techniques like DNA analysis has transformed investigations. DNA analysis, which became widespread in the 1980s, led to groundbreaking case resolutions. One notable case was that of Colin Pitchfork, the first person convicted of murder based on genetic evidence.

Today, technology underpins every investigation. Modern databases like CODIS in the U.S. allow investigators to rapidly compare fingerprints, DNA profiles, and other evidence against massive data resources. Additionally, digital investigations can now analyze internet histories, social media activity, and cellphone locations, providing investigators with powerful new ways to track criminals.

- Contemporary Crime: New Challenges for Media and Technology

In the 21st century, the internet has transformed both crime and the methods for combating it. Cybercrime, or crimes committed online, requires law enforcement to adopt new tools and skills to keep up with offenders. Social media also plays an increasing role in investigations, both as a source of information about suspects and as a platform for exposing them.

Media and technology are invaluable tools for investigators but also present challenges. Society increasingly expects rapid and dramatic results in criminal investigations, placing greater pressure on law enforcement agencies. Yet it's thanks to technological advancements and media support that forensics has reached a level that was unimaginable just a few decades ago.

3. Famous Criminal Cases

- ## Ted Bundy: The Killer Next Door

Ted Bundy is one of the most notorious serial killers of the 20th century. His story is both terrifying and fascinating—Bundy skillfully masked his true nature, coming across as a handsome, charismatic, and intelligent young man. This facade enabled him to gain his victims' trust before revealing his murderous side.

- ## The Making of a Monster

Bundy was born on November 24, 1946, in Burlington, Vermont. His early life was chaotic—he was raised believing that his grandparents were his parents and that his mother was his sister. Although his adult life appeared orderly, the first signs of his deviance were already emerging. Bundy gradually developed a manipulative skillset, learning to deceive people and conceal his dark inclinations.

His criminal career began in the early 1970s when he started abducting, raping, and murdering young women across several U.S. states. Surprisingly, Bundy avoided suspicion for a long time—he was politically active, studied law, and even worked in the governor's office. His clean-cut, responsible image made him even more dangerous.

- ## How Bundy Hunted His Victims

Ted Bundy was a master manipulator. He often pretended to be injured, using a sling on his arm or a cast on his leg to gain sympathy. He would approach young women, asking for help carrying items to his car. Once he gained their trust, he would abduct and brutally murder them. Many witnesses described him as charming and polite, underscoring his ability to mask his true, dark nature.

Bundy operated in multiple states, complicating the investigation. By the time authorities connected the crimes, he had already moved on to another location. His primary hunting grounds were Washington, Utah, Colorado, and Florida. His victims were mostly young women, often students with long, dark hair—a feature that some believe reminded him of a former girlfriend who broke off their engagement.

- ## Trials and Escapes

Bundy was eventually arrested in Utah in 1975 for driving without headlights. A search of his car revealed suspicious items like a crowbar, handcuffs, and a mask, raising police suspicions. But Bundy didn't intend to go down easily—after being arrested, he managed to escape from jail twice. The most spectacular was his 1977 escape from a Colorado jail; he evaded capture for two months before reaching Florida, where he resumed his killing spree.

In Florida, Bundy committed some of his most brutal murders, including the killing of two women in a university dormitory and another student just days later. Finally, he was arrested again in 1978, and his trial attracted massive media attention.

- The Media and His Trial

Ted Bundy's trial became one of the first media spectacles centered on a serial killer. Bundy represented himself in court, an unusual move, especially in such a serious case. Despite being accused of heinous murders, his charisma and manipulative abilities won him a surprising number of admirers, particularly among women. Some believe that Bundy deliberately used his appearance and the media to manipulate public perception.

Bundy was ultimately sentenced to death, and in 1989, he was executed in Florida's electric chair. Even in his final days, he tried to delay execution by offering new information about his crimes.

- Bundy's Legacy

Ted Bundy killed at least 30 women, though some sources suggest the victim count may be higher. His story still horrifies and fascinates people today—how could a man with such looks and charisma be so ruthless?

Bundy became the embodiment of hidden evil—a monster lurking behind a mask of "normalcy." His case inspired countless books, films, and documentaries, and his name became synonymous with "serial killer." His skillful manipulation, intelligence, and cold-blooded cruelty make him one of the most terrifying criminals in history.

The Zodiac Case: An Unsolved Mystery

One of the most mysterious and terrifying cases in the history of forensics is the Zodiac case—a serial killer who terrorized California in the 1960s and 70s. Despite numerous attempts to identify him and a wealth of evidence, the Zodiac's true identity remains unknown. His cryptic letters, ciphers, and brutal murders have made him one of the most famous unsolved cases in history.

- The Zodiac Murders

The first attacks attributed to the Zodiac occurred in 1968. On a highway near Vallejo, California, a young couple—Betty Lou Jensen and David Faraday—was shot while sitting in their car. The police had no suspects or motive at the time, and the case went cold.

Months later, in July 1969, there was another brutal attack. Another couple—Darlene Ferrin and Michael Mageau—was shot in their car, but this time Michael survived. Following this attack, the police received their first direct contact from the killer: a man called the station and confessed to both crimes, providing details only the perpetrator could know.

In August 1969, three California newspapers received letters from someone calling himself "The Zodiac." In these letters, he described his crimes and included complex ciphers that he claimed would reveal his identity. The Zodiac threatened to kill more people if the letters weren't published.

- ## Ciphers and Mysterious Letters

One of the most distinct elements of the Zodiac case was his communication with the media and police. The Zodiac sent encrypted messages to newspapers that supposedly contained clues to his identity. The first cipher was cracked by an amateur cryptography couple, but instead of revealing his name, it contained an eerie message: "I like killing because it is so much fun."

The Zodiac continued to send ciphers, some of which remain unsolved to this day. Each letter taunted the police with challenges, and his confidence grew with each murder.

In October 1969, the Zodiac murdered a cab driver, Paul Stine, in San Francisco. This time, the investigation came closer than ever—witnesses saw the killer, and the police collected fingerprints and other evidence from the crime scene. However, despite these leads, the Zodiac evaded capture.

- ## Who Was the Zodiac?

There are many theories about the Zodiac's identity. One of the main suspects was Arthur Leigh Allen, a California teacher who matched the Zodiac's profile. Although Allen was under surveillance and had some connections to the case, there wasn't enough evidence to charge him.

Another theory speculated that the Zodiac might have been more than one person, a group acting together to mislead the police. Some researchers suggested that the killer may have had military or intelligence ties, given his knowledge of cryptography.

In the 1970s, the murders suddenly stopped, but the Zodiac continued to send letters, sparking speculation that he may have stopped killing or had possibly died. The last confirmed letter from the Zodiac arrived in 1974. Although his activities ceased, the Zodiac case was never closed, and investigators continue to examine new evidence.

- ## The Legacy of the Zodiac

The Zodiac case remains one of the most captivating and frightening unsolved investigations. A killer who toyed with police and the media has become a symbol of hidden evil and unmatched manipulative skills. His letters and ciphers continue to intrigue and fuel theories, and researchers worldwide are still trying to unmask him.

The Zodiac has inspired numerous books, films, and television series, and his persona still captivates researchers and conspiracy enthusiasts alike. With the aid of modern technologies like DNA analysis, there is hope that the Zodiac's mystery might one day be solved. For now, his story remains one of the most enigmatic in the history of crime.

Jeffrey Dahmer: The Milwaukee Cannibal

Jeffrey Dahmer, known as the "Milwaukee Cannibal," is one of the most horrifying figures in the history of serial killers. His crimes were so brutal and gruesome that they shocked even the most seasoned investigators. Dahmer didn't just murder his victims—he dismembered them and kept their body parts, which he later consumed. His story exemplifies the darkest side of human psychology, compounded by systemic failures that allowed one of the most chilling murder sprees in U.S. history.

- ## Early Life and the Birth of a Killer

Jeffrey Dahmer was born on May 21, 1960, in Milwaukee, Wisconsin. From a young age, he showed disturbing tendencies—fascinated with dead animals he found, Dahmer would perform "dissections" on them. He was a loner, quiet and withdrawn, which worried his family, though his true problems wouldn't emerge until later.

Dahmer committed his first murder in 1978, at just 18 years old. His victim, 18-year-old Steven Hicks, was invited into Dahmer's home, where he was subsequently strangled. Dahmer dismembered Hicks' body and concealed the remains in his home. Although this murder could have been a one-time event, Dahmer quickly discovered that killing gave him a sense of control and power, fueling his murderous instincts.

- ## A Horrific Killing Spree

After a brief hiatus, Dahmer resumed killing in 1987, beginning with his second victim, Steven Tuomi. This marked a new, more brutal phase in his activities. Dahmer began preying on young men he met in gay bars, inviting them back to his apartment where he drugged, killed, and dismembered them.

His methods grew increasingly horrifying. Dahmer not only killed his victims but also preserved their skulls and kept parts of their bodies, such as hearts and muscles, in his refrigerator to consume later. These grisly practices earned him the nickname "The Milwaukee Cannibal."

One of Dahmer's most disturbing tactics was his attempt to create "living zombies." He injected acid or other chemicals directly into the brains of some victims, hoping to leave them in a submissive, yet living state. These experiments were unsuccessful, and their brutality is difficult to fathom.

- ## Arrest and Trial

Dahmer operated with impunity for years, largely due to investigative oversights. In 1991, police had an opportunity to intervene when Dahmer's neighbors called officers to his apartment, where they found a drugged, semi-nude teenage boy, Konerak Sinthasomphone. Dahmer convinced the officers that the boy was his boyfriend and that they were simply having a domestic dispute. Unaware of what was happening inside, the police left, effectively sealing Sinthasomphone's fate, as Dahmer murdered him shortly afterward.

Dahmer was finally apprehended in July 1991, when his intended victim, Tracy Edwards, managed to escape and led police back to Dahmer's apartment. Inside, officers found a horrific scene: photographs of dismembered bodies, containers holding human remains, and tools used for dismemberment.

During his trial, Dahmer confessed to killing 17 men and boys between 1978 and 1991. His testimonies were extraordinarily graphic, solidifying his status as one of the most infamous serial killers in history. Despite an insanity defense, Dahmer was found guilty and sentenced to multiple life terms.

- ## Death Behind Bars and Legacy

Jeffrey Dahmer's time in prison was brief. In November 1994, he was murdered by a fellow inmate, Christopher Scarver, who attacked Dahmer during a work detail in the prison. Some theories suggest that the attack was deliberate, as Scarver believed Dahmer's brutal crimes rendered him unworthy of life.

Dahmer remains a figure of both horror and morbid fascination. His crimes have been the subject of numerous books, films, and documentaries, highlighting the severe oversights by law enforcement and the judicial system that enabled him to operate unchecked for so long.

Jeffrey Dahmer stands as one of history's most notorious serial killers, a reminder of the horrifying evil that can hide behind an "ordinary" exterior. His crimes reveal the depths to which a human mind can descend into darkness.

Charles Manson: Cult, Manipulation, and Murder

Charles Manson is one of the most controversial figures in criminal history—a man who not only became a serial killer but also led a cult that he manipulated into committing horrifying murders. Manson didn't act alone; he used his dark influence over his followers to drive them to crimes that shocked America in the late 1960s. His actions contributed to the decline of the "flower child" era and left deep scars on American culture.

- The Birth of a Cult: Manson's "Family"

Manson had a troubled childhood and youth, growing up in reform schools and spending many years in prison for petty crimes. But it was his actions after being released in the 1960s that made his name synonymous with evil.

Manson formed a cult known as "The Family," a group of mostly young women who were captivated by his charisma and believed in his visions. Manson presented himself as a prophet, claiming he would lead his followers through apocalyptic times he insisted were inevitable. His ideas were heavily influenced by music—particularly songs by The Beatles—and New Age mysticism. One of his core beliefs was that a "race war," which he called "Helter Skelter" (after The Beatles' song), was imminent and would end with him seizing power over the world.

The Manson Family settled on a secluded ranch in California, where Manson used psychological terror and manipulation to turn his followers into obedient tools. He used drugs, especially LSD, and emotional abuse to maintain control over them, often keeping them in a trance-like state.

- Helter Skelter: Apocalyptic Vision and Murder

Manson convinced his followers that a racial war was unavoidable and that they had to incite it. He believed that a series of brutal murders could spark panic and pin blame on the Black Panther Party, leading to the racial revolution he prophesied.

On the night of August 8, 1969, members of the Family—Susan Atkins, Tex Watson, Patricia Krenwinkel, and Linda Kasabian—acted on Manson's orders and went to the home at 10050 Cielo Drive in Beverly Hills, which belonged to director Roman Polanski. Polanski was out of the country, but his pregnant wife, actress Sharon Tate, was there with her friends Jay Sebring, Abigail Folger, and Wojciech Frykowski.

Under Manson's direction, the cult members broke into the home and brutally murdered everyone present. Tate, who pleaded for the life of her unborn child, was savagely killed by Susan Atkins. The attackers smeared words like "PIG" in the victims' blood on the walls.

The following night, the group attacked again, this time targeting a random couple, Leno and Rosemary LaBianca, who were murdered in their home. Manson and his followers believed these murders would kick-start the racial revolution that, of course, never came.

- ## Arrest and Trial

Although the Manson Family initially evaded justice, Susan Atkins eventually boasted about the murders to other inmates while in jail for a separate crime. This confession led detectives to unravel the Cielo Drive murders. After an extensive investigation, Charles Manson and his followers were arrested and brought to trial.

The Manson trial became a media spectacle. Manson, with his distinctive "X" carved into his forehead (later modified to a swastika), and his followers, who adopted the same symbol, did everything possible to turn the proceedings into a circus. They frequently disrupted the court, and Manson tried to persuade the court of his apocalyptic beliefs. Despite not committing the murders himself, Manson was found guilty for orchestrating the crimes.

In 1971, Manson and several of his followers were sentenced to death. However, when California temporarily abolished the death penalty, their sentences were commuted to life imprisonment. Manson spent the rest of his life in prison, where he gained a following who saw him as a symbol of countercultural rebellion.

- ## Manson's Legacy

Charles Manson died in prison in 2017, but his legacy endures. His influence and manipulation of his followers shocked society, and the murders of Sharon Tate and the other Manson Family victims marked the end of the "innocent" 1960s. Manson became a symbol of manipulation, the dark side of countercultural movements, and the dangers that can arise from a mix of charisma and insanity.

His story continues to inspire countless books, films, and documentaries, and he remains one of America's most infamous and controversial criminals. His ability to control people to the point of committing horrific crimes serves as a chilling reminder of how far the human mind can descend into darkness.

Other Crimes That Shocked the World

The Lindbergh Case: The Kidnapping of a "National Hero's" Child

One of the most notorious cases of the 20th century occurred in 1932 when Charles Lindbergh Jr., son of famed aviator Charles Lindbergh, was kidnapped from the family home in New Jersey. Lindbergh was a national hero, celebrated for being the first to fly solo across the Atlantic, and the kidnapping of his child caused a massive media frenzy.

The kidnappers demanded a large ransom, but even after it was paid, the child was never returned. Weeks later, his body was found in the woods only a few miles from the Lindbergh home.

Following an extensive investigation and media circus, Bruno Richard Hauptmann was arrested in 1934 and charged with the child's kidnapping and murder. Dubbed the "trial of the century," the proceedings captured global attention. Hauptmann was found guilty and sentenced to death, though to this day, many question his guilt, making the Lindbergh case one of the most controversial in judicial history.

- The JonBenét Ramsey Case: Murder in the Spotlight

The 1996 murder of six-year-old JonBenét Ramsey in Boulder, Colorado, is one of America's most puzzling and widely publicized cases. JonBenét, a child beauty pageant contestant, was found strangled in the basement of her family's home the day after Christmas. Alongside her body, a ransom note was found, though no actual kidnapping occurred.

The JonBenét case quickly drew global media attention. Initial suspicions fell on the family—parents and brother—but despite numerous theories, the true culprit has never been identified.

The unsolved circumstances, intense media coverage, and investigative errors turned the JonBenét case into a symbol of unresolved crime. Despite years of investigation and efforts to close the case, the killer of JonBenét Ramsey remains unknown.

- The O.J. Simpson Case: A Crime and Trial That Divided America

The O.J. Simpson case is among the most famous and divisive criminal investigations in history. In 1994, former football star and celebrity O.J. Simpson was charged with the murders of his ex-wife, Nicole Brown Simpson, and her friend Ron Goldman. The crime's brutality, Simpson's fame, and his dramatic escape from police (captured in the infamous white Ford Bronco chase) turned the trial into a media spectacle watched by millions worldwide.

The trial, which lasted 11 months, divided the U.S. Simpson's defense team skillfully challenged the evidence, accusing the police of procedural errors and racial bias. In October 1995, Simpson was acquitted, sparking widespread controversy and protests. The case remains a potent symbol of racial and social divides in America.

- The Murder of Gianni Versace: Celebrity Killer

In 1997, the fashion world was rocked by the murder of Gianni Versace, one of the most celebrated designers. Versace was fatally shot on the steps of his Miami Beach home by Andrew Cunanan, a spree killer who had already murdered four others.

Cunanan, driven by obsessive hatred and psychological instability, evaded law enforcement for months before committing suicide on a boat in Florida shortly after killing Versace. Although investigators never confirmed a specific motive for Versace's murder, speculation surrounding Cunanan's psychological state and Versace's private life led to numerous theories.

The killing of Gianni Versace inspired various books, films, and television series, including the popular American Crime Story. This case highlights the precarious line between fame and criminality, revealing the dark underside of celebrity culture.

4. Crime Puzzles and Quizzes

Do You Know the Facts? – Crime Quiz

Crime has fascinated people for years, but how much do you really know about the most infamous criminal cases? This quiz is a great opportunity to test your knowledge about murders, serial killers, and investigations. Answer the questions below and see if you can crack these criminal mysteries.

1. Who was the first serial killer in U.S. history, known for the "Murder Castle"?

    a) Ted Bundy

    b) H.H. Holmes

    c) Jeffrey Dahmer

    d) John Wayne Gacy

2. Which famous murder shocked Hollywood in 1969 and was linked to Charles Manson's cult?

    a) Marilyn Monroe's death

    b) Sharon Tate's murder

    c) Grace Kelly's death

    d) James Dean's case

3. Which serial killer sent taunting letters to newspapers and was never caught?

    a) Jack the Ripper

    b) Zodiac

    c) Richard Ramirez

    d) Dennis Rader (BTK)

4. Which type of forensic analysis revolutionized criminal investigations in the 1980s?

a) Fingerprinting

b) DNA analysis

c) Ballistics

d) Blood analysis

5. In what year was Charles Lindbergh's son kidnapped in the case known as the "Crime of the Century"?

a) 1928

b) 1932

c) 1940

d) 1951

6. Which serial killer survived acquittal but later confessed to murdering 33 boys and young men, hiding their bodies in his home's crawlspace?

a) Jeffrey Dahmer

b) John Wayne Gacy

c) Ted Bundy

d) Albert Fish

7. What nickname was given to Richard Ramirez, the serial killer who terrorized California in the 1980s?

a) Night Stalker

b) Green River Killer

c) Angel of Death

d) BTK Killer

Match the Perpetrator to the Crime

Each serial killer has a unique modus operandi, and some criminal cases have gone down in history due to the distinct methods of their perpetrators. Can you match the infamous criminals to their notorious crimes? Test your knowledge!

Instructions: Below is a list of crimes and a list of perpetrators. Your task is to match each crime with the appropriate criminal. Let's see how well you know these notorious figures!

Crimes:

Murder of female students in a Florida dormitory

Murder and burial of 33 young men under a house

Series of murders on young couples near San Francisco, accompanied by encrypted messages to the press

Strangling of several women, whose bodies were found near a lake in Seattle

Kidnapping and murder of a famous American aviator's son

Killing young gay men, keeping body parts in a refrigerator

Brutal murder of actress Sharon Tate and friends in Beverly Hills

Perpetrators:

a) Ted Bundy

b) Zodiac

c) Charles Manson

d) Jeffrey Dahmer

e) John Wayne Gacy

f) Bruno Richard Hauptmann

g) Richard Ramirez (Night Stalker)

Solutions:

- Murder of female students in a Florida dormitory – a) Ted Bundy
- Ted Bundy killed two female students in a Florida State University dorm in 1978, shortly before his final arrest.
- Murder and burial of 33 young men under a house – e) John Wayne Gacy
- Gacy killed 33 young men and boys, burying their bodies in the crawlspace of his Chicago home.
- Series of murders on young couples near San Francisco, accompanied by encrypted messages to the press – b) Zodiac
- The Zodiac killer targeted young couples and sent encrypted messages to newspapers, taunting the police and hinting at his identity.
- Strangling of several women, whose bodies were found near a lake in Seattle – a) Ted Bundy
- Ted Bundy targeted young women in Washington and Utah, with several victims found near Lake Sammamish.
- Kidnapping and murder of a famous American aviator's son – f) Bruno Richard Hauptmann
- Hauptmann was convicted of kidnapping and murdering Charles Lindbergh's son, in what was dubbed the "crime of the century" in the 1930s.
- Killing young gay men, keeping body parts in a refrigerator – d) Jeffrey Dahmer
- Dahmer murdered his victims, dismembered them, and kept body parts in his refrigerator.
- Brutal murder of actress Sharon Tate and friends in Beverly Hills – c) Charles Manson
- Manson's followers murdered Sharon Tate and others in 1969 under his orders, in a crime that shocked the nation.

Fact or Fiction? Distinguish Real Crimes from Myths

Movies, books, and rumors often blur the lines between truth and fiction, making it hard to tell fact from myth. Can you differentiate real crimes from fictionalized tales? Test your intuition and knowledge!

Questions:

- The Zodiac killer was caught and sentenced to life in the 1990s.

  Fact or Fiction?

- Jeffrey Dahmer was a surgeon before he began his killing spree.

  Fact or Fiction?

- Ted Bundy escaped from jail twice before finally being captured.

  Fact or Fiction?

- Charles Manson personally committed the murders of Sharon Tate and her friends.

  Fact or Fiction?

- H.H. Holmes built a hotel filled with traps where he killed his victims.

  Fact or Fiction?

- John Wayne Gacy was active in California at the same time as Richard Ramirez.

  Fact or Fiction?

- Albert Fish sent a letter to the family of one of his victims, detailing the murder.

  Fact or Fiction?

Solutions:

- Fiction – The Zodiac killer was never caught or sentenced, and his identity remains unknown to this day.

- Fiction – Dahmer was not a surgeon. Although his methods of dismemberment led some to assume he had medical knowledge, this was not the case.

- Fact – Ted Bundy did escape twice: once by jumping from a library window and another time by crawling through a ceiling panel in his cell.

- Fiction – Manson didn't personally commit the murders but instructed his followers to do so.

- Fact – H.H. Holmes built the "Murder Castle" with secret passageways, traps, and soundproof rooms where he killed his victims.

- Fiction – John Wayne Gacy operated in Chicago, while Richard Ramirez, the Night Stalker, was active in California.

- Fact – Albert Fish sent a gruesome letter to the family of one of his victims, describing the murder and acts of cannibalism.

Who Am I? – Quiz Based on Descriptions of Infamous Criminals

Identify these notorious criminals based on their stories. Here are new descriptions covering various types of crimes, from serial murders to large-scale criminal operations. Can you match each description with the right criminal?

Descriptions:

- I was one of the few female serial killers. I killed seven men between 1989 and 1990, claiming all my crimes were acts of self-defense. My story inspired the movie Monster. Who am I?

- I was responsible for murdering over 50 women and children in the USSR during the 1970s and 80s. Known as the "Butcher of Rostov," I was eventually caught and sentenced to death despite attempts to hide my crimes. Who am I?

- I am one of the most wanted men in the world, the leader of the Sinaloa drug cartel. I escaped from prison multiple times, and my cartel is responsible for widespread violence and drug trafficking worldwide. Who am I?

- My kidnapping in 1974 shocked the world, but even more surprising was that I joined the group that abducted me, participating in bank robberies. My story sparked controversy over brainwashing and loyalty. Who am I?

- I am one of the last "elusive" Sicilian mafia bosses, known for brutal attacks on government officials and controlling vast areas of criminal activity in Italy. Though hunted for decades, I evaded capture for a long time. Who am I?

- I killed dozens of young men in the 1970s and hid their bodies in the crawlspace of my home. I worked as a clown at children's parties, making my crimes all the more shocking. Who am I?

- I inspired the movies Silence of the Lambs and Psycho with my gruesome crimes. Collecting trophies from my victims and using them for horrifying purposes made me one of the most terrifying criminals of the 20th century. Who am I?

Solutions:

- Aileen Wuornos – She killed seven men, claiming self-defense, and her story inspired the movie Monster.

- Andrei Chikatilo – The "Butcher of Rostov" murdered over 50 women and children in the USSR, and was caught and sentenced to death in the 1990s.

- Joaquín "El Chapo" Guzmán – Leader of the Sinaloa cartel, known for multiple prison escapes and involvement in large-scale drug trafficking.

- Patty Hearst – Kidnapped in 1974, she later joined her captors, the Symbionese Liberation Army, sparking debates about brainwashing.

- Matteo Messina Denaro – A Sicilian mafia boss and fugitive for decades, known for his brutal tactics and connections to Cosa Nostra.

- John Wayne Gacy – The "Killer Clown," who murdered 33 young men and hid their bodies in his home's crawlspace.

- Ed Gein – Inspired characters in Silence of the Lambs and Psycho. His practice of collecting trophies from bodies made him a notorious figure in criminal history.

Crime-Themed Puzzles and Brain Teasers

How to Solve: Criminal Wordsearch

In this crime-themed wordsearch, your mission is to uncover hidden words linked to various facets of forensics, criminal profiling, and notorious cases. Words like evidence, witness, profile, and trace are woven into the puzzle, waiting for you to find them. Look carefully in all directions—horizontal, vertical, and diagonal—as each term can appear forwards or backwards. Challenge your observation skills and immerse yourself in the intriguing world of forensic investigation!

Crime Scene

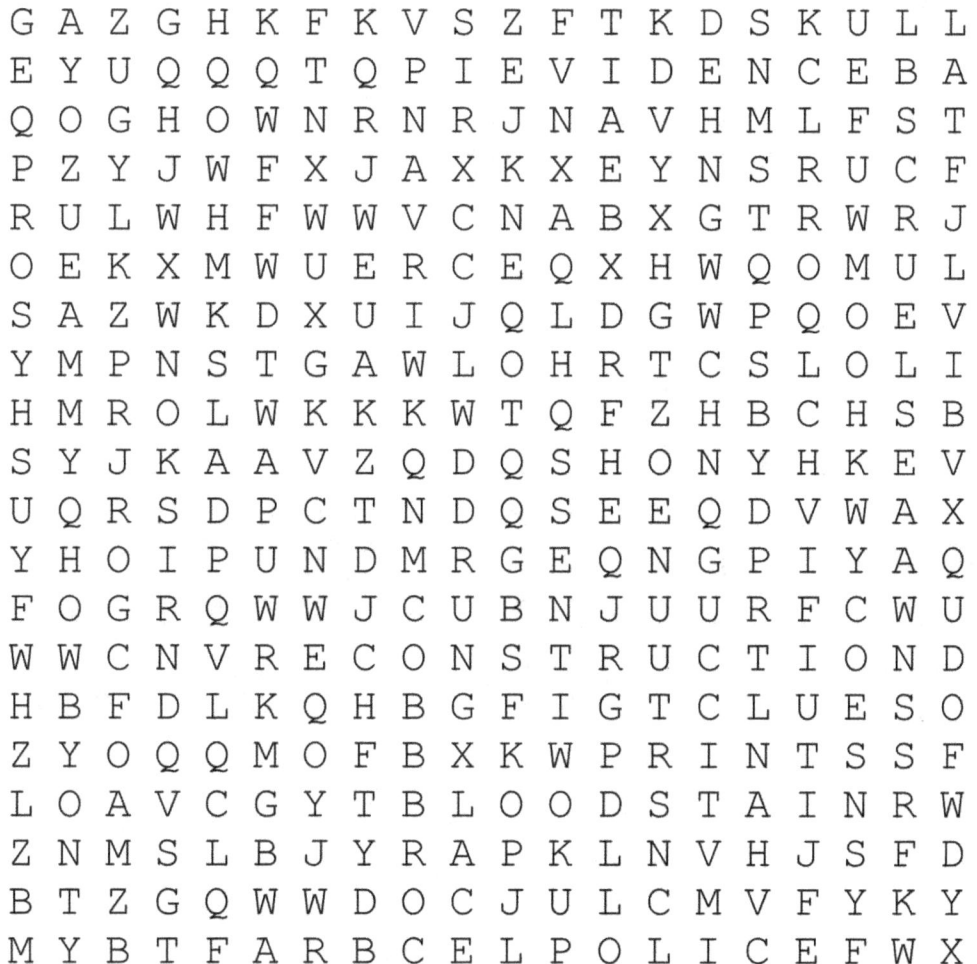

1. Evidence 2. Trace 3. Witness 4. Police 5. Reconstruction
6. Skull 7. Bloodstain 8. Tool 9. Prints 10. Clues

Criminal Profiling

```
O Y E E E A G W A V M J W K L X Z E W J
A N G T M E M Y I Y P S Y C H O L O G Y
G T X C C M W O R P K W Q R K A S J H E
G R K A P O Z E T Q U I Q I Q R S L U R
R A U R R T O E Z I P T I C B P L T Y V
E U C S E I M Q R O V D O O R J X V D R
S M O M T O Z J K Y T E O T O G F Z C F
S A G B C N T A T O C Y U W I P S G A Z
I G H K A S F K V S Z Y F T V K H D E Y
O U Q Q R Q Q P I B A S Q O A G O H O W
N N N R A J N A V H M U L F H S C T P Z
Y J W F H X J X K X E O Y N E S K R U C
F R U L C W H F W W V L N A B B X G R W
R J O E K X M W U E R A C Q X H W Q M U
B L S A Z W K D X U I E J Q L D G W P Q
E V Y M P N S T G A W J L O H R T C S L
O I H M R O L W K K K W T Q F Z H B C H
S B S Y J K A A V Z Q D Q H O N Y H K E
V U Q R S D P C T N D Q E E Q D V W A X
Y H O I P U N D M R G R E V E N G E Q N
```

1. Psychology 2. Motive 3. Jealousy 4. Revenge 5. Character
6. Aggression 7. Trauma 8. Emotions 9. Behavior 10. Shock

Forensic Tools

```
V M O Y E E E A G W A V M J W K L X Z E
T U B E W J L N G T M I C R O S C O P E
C M Y I Y X C U C W R P K W Q R K A S J
A H E K A P Z E M Q U I Q I Q R S L U R
M U R O E Z P T I I C B P L T Y V C S M
E Q R O D O O J X V N D R O M Z J K Y T
R O T G Y F Z C F G B O T A T O C Y U W
A P G A S Z G H K F K V L S Z F T K D E
Y U Q B P Q Q Q P I B A Q O G H O W N N
R J N L O A V H M L F L S T P Z Y J W F
X J X O T K X E Y N S E R U C F R U L W
H F W O U W V N A B G P R W R J O E K X
M W U D A E R C Q X H L W Q M U L S A Z
W K D U I J Q L D G W A P Q E V E Y M P
N S T G A W L O H R T C C S L O C I H M
R O L W K K K W T L Q S F Z H B A C H S
B S Y J K A A V Z Q E D Q H O N R Y H K
E V U Q R S D P C T N N D Q E E T Q D V
W A X Y H O I P U N D M S R G Q N G P I
Y A Q F O G R Q W W J P R I N T C U B J
```

1. Microscope   **2.** Luminol   **3.** Scalpel   **4.** Print   **5.** Autopsy
6. Tube   **7.** Camera   **8.** Blood   **9.** Trace   **10.** Lens

Criminals and Crimes

```
P J P H Q J V M O Y E E E A G W A V M J
W K L X Z E R W J N T H I E F G T M B Y
C I Y X C C W O R P K W Q R K A S J U H
E A K A P Z E Q B U I Q I Q R S L U R R
U R N O E Z P T I B C B P L T Y V C G S
M Q R N O D O O J X E V D R O M Z J L K
Y T O T I G F Z C F G R B T A T O C A Y
U W G A R B Z G H K F L Y K V S Z F R T
K D E K E Y A U Q Q Q I Q P I B A Q Y O
G H O I G W N L N R J A N A V H M L F S
T P Z D R Y J W F X J M K X K X R E Y N
S R U N O C F R U L W K I H F W E W V N
A B X A F G R W R J O C D E K X R M W U
E R C P Q X H W Q M U A N B L S E A Z W
K D X P U I J Q L D G L A W P Q D E V Y
M P N I S T G A W L O B P H R T R C S L
O I H N M R O L W K K K P W T Q U F Z H
B C H G S B S Y J K A A E V Z Q M D Q H
O N Y H K E V U Q R S D R P C T N D Q E
E Q D V W A Y H O I P F R A U D U N D M
```

1. Thief **2.** Robbery **3.** Blackmail **4.** Fraud **5.** Forger
6. Burglary **7.** Kidnapper **8.** Cannibal **9.** Kidnapping **10.** Murderer

Famous Investigations

```
H Q J V M O Y E E E A G W A V M J W K L
X Z E W J E T N G T C A S E M E Y I Y X
C C W R P K V R W Q R K A S J L H E K A
P Z E Q U I Q I I I Q R S L U I R U R O
E Z P T I C B P D A L T Y V Y F C S M Q
R O D O O J X V D E L R O M N O Z J K Y
T O T G F Z C F G B N T A T O R O C Y U
W P G A Z G H K F K V C S Z M P F T K D
E Y U Q Q Q Q P I B A Q E O I G H O W N
N R J N A V H M L F S T P Z T Y J W F X
J X K X E Y N S R U C F R C S U L W H F
I N T E R R O G A T I O N H E W W V N A
B X G R W R J O E K X M W E T U E R C Q
X H W Q M U L S A Z W K D S X U I J Q L
D G W P Q E V Y M P N S T S G A W L O H
R T C S L O I H M R O C I B L W K K K W
T Q F Z H B C H S B S O B O Y J K A A V
Z Q D Q H O N Y H K E U I A V U Q R S D
P C T N D Q E E Q D V R L R W A X Y H O
I P U N D M R G Q N G T A D P I Y A Q F
```

1. Case **2.** Trial **3.** Court **4.** Alibi **5.** Interrogation
6. Chessboard **7.** Profile **8.** Evidence **9.** Testimony

Murderer's Ciphers: Cryptograms

Below are five cryptograms with encrypted messages from a fictional "criminal." Each cipher is paired with a key to help you crack the code and uncover the message. Instructions for decoding are given for each cipher type, and solutions are listed at the end.

- ## How to Solve the Ciphers

- Caesar Cipher – In this type of cipher, each letter of the message is shifted left or right by a specified number of places in the alphabet. For example, if the key says "shift 2 right," then the letter "A" becomes "C." Apply this shift individually to each letter according to the given key.

- Numeric Cipher – Each number in the cipher corresponds to a letter in the alphabet: A=1, B=2, C=3, and so forth. Convert each number into its letter to reveal the hidden message.

- Letter Transposition – Letters in the message are scrambled in a specific pattern. The key will tell you how to rearrange the letters, e.g., by taking every second letter in order from the start to end, then starting from the beginning again.

- Reverse Caesar Cipher – A variation of the Caesar Cipher, this requires a shift to the right instead of the typical left. Apply the given shift to each letter individually to reveal the message.

- Symbol Substitution – Symbols are used to represent letters in this cipher. Use the key provided to substitute symbols with the correct letters.

Cryptograms to Solve

Caesar Cipher

Message: "VJG UCTG FGDKCNF"

Key: Shift 2 letters to the left.

....

Numeric Cipher

Message: "4-9-18-5-3-20"

Key: Each number corresponds to a letter in the alphabet (A=1, B=2, etc.).

Letter Transposition

Message: "HET LIELR SOFTEH EVDINCEE"

Key: Rearrange by taking every third letter from start to end, then loop back.

....

Reverse Caesar Cipher

Message: "OWMQHKZXV"

Key: Shift 4 letters to the right.

Symbol Substitution

Message: "□△✱□✪ △✦□★"

Key: Symbols correspond to letters in the following order: □=C, △=R, ✱=I, ✪=M, ✦=E, ★=S

Solutions

Caesar Cipher

Message: "VJG UCTG FGDKCNF"

Key: Shift 2 letters to the left.

Answer: "THE SAFE DETAILS"

Numeric Cipher

Message: "4-9-18-5-3-20"

Key: Each number corresponds to a letter in the alphabet.

Answer: "DIRECT"

Letter Transposition

Message: "HET LIELR SOFTEH EVDINCEE"

Key: Rearrange by taking every third letter from start to end, then loop back.

Answer: "THE KILLER LEFT HINTS"

Reverse Caesar Cipher

Message: "OWMQHKZXV"

Key: Shift 4 letters to the right.

Answer: "SECRET CODE"

Symbol Substitution

Message: "□△✱ □✪ △✦□★"

Key: Symbols correspond to letters in the following order: □=C, △=R, ✱=I, ✪=M, ✦=E, ★=S

Answer: "CRIME SCENE"

Criminal Crosswords

Below you'll find 20 descriptions related to the world of criminology. The "Answer" space has dots where you'll need to fill in the correct terms based on each description. The answers are numbered at the end. Good luck!

Descriptions:

1. A technique for identifying criminals using fingerprints.
Answer: ......

2. Device used to detect blood traces invisible to the naked eye.
Answer: ......

3. Infamous 19th-century London serial killer who was never caught.
Answer: ......

4. The process of psychological analysis and behavior reconstruction to determine a perpetrator's profile.
Answer: ......

5. Forensic tool used to examine bullet structure and origins as well as firearms.
Answer: ......

6. Material from which DNA samples, such as hair, saliva, or blood, are collected to identify suspects.
Answer: ......

7. Device for recording video, monitoring public or private spaces to prevent crime.
Answer: ......

8. Traces collected by police from clothing or surfaces after contact by the perpetrator or victim.
Answer: ......

9. Chemical analysis that identifies the presence and type of drugs, toxins, or other chemicals.
Answer: ......

10. A method used to gather information on a suspect's contact with firearms through gunpowder residue on skin.
Answer: ......

11. Famous substance used by forensic scientists that glows when it contacts blood.

Answer: ......

12. Location where the victim's body and other potential evidence, such as blood or fingerprints, are found.
Answer: ......

13. Device that detects movement at a crime scene or monitors suspicious areas.
Answer: ......

14. Process of collecting and analyzing data on a suspect's movements or calls via cell signals.
Answer: ......

15. Medical technique used to determine cause of death and time of death, typically conducted post-mortem.
Answer: ......

16. Specialized report identifying the type of wounds and tools used during the crime.
Answer: ......

17. Type of analysis that allows investigators to determine height, direction, and force of blood spatters.
Answer: ......

18. Crime scene investigation method analyzing trace locations and types to recreate the sequence of events.
Answer: ......

19. Technique for extracting DNA from objects or samples of biological material.
Answer: ......

20. Specialized forensic field focused on examining explosion traces, explosives, and flammable substances.
Answer: ......

Answers:

1. Fingerprinting
2. Luminol
3. Jack the Ripper
4. Profiling
5. Ballistics
6. Biological material
7. Surveillance camera
8. Fibers
9. Spectrometry
10. Gunpowder residue
11. Luminol
12. Crime scene
13. Motion sensor
14. Cell signal analysis
15. Autopsy
16. Medical report
17. Blood spatter analysis
18. Crime scene reconstruction
19. DNA isolation
20. Explosives expertise

Each of these terms represents an element of investigation that could be crucial to solving a case. Understanding these techniques and terms brings us closer to the methods used by detectives and forensic experts.

5. Criminal Profiling

What is Criminal Profiling?

Criminal profiling is a fascinating field of forensics that blends psychology with investigative science to create a psychological profile of an unknown offender. The aim of profiling is to understand who the criminal is by examining clues left at the crime scene, behavioral patterns, and the psychological motives driving their actions.

Criminal profiling involves analyzing patterns in the offender's behavior. Investigators create a psychological profile that includes information on the likely age, gender, education, life experiences, and methods used by the criminal. This tool helps narrow down the suspect pool and offers insight into the offender's motivations.

- ### Types of Offenders: Organized and Disorganized

A key concept in profiling is the division between organized and disorganized offenders. An organized offender acts methodically, plans crimes in advance, is often intelligent, and takes care not to leave evidence behind. Ted Bundy, for instance, serves as an example of an organized offender, as he carefully selected and manipulated his victims.

A disorganized offender, on the other hand, acts impulsively, often without a plan, typically in a state of emotional excitement. Their crimes are chaotic, and the crime scene is likely to be full of evidence. Richard Ramirez, known as the "Night Stalker," exemplifies a disorganized offender, with crimes that were highly violent and often unpredictable.

- ### A Tool for Investigators

Profiling isn't a flawless method for identifying criminals, but it's an invaluable tool for investigators. Psychologists and profilers frequently collaborate with detectives, analyzing not only physical evidence but also the emotions and motivations behind the crime. This approach helps anticipate how an offender may behave in the future, where they might strike next, and what habits or routines they may exhibit.

The History of Profiling: From the FBI to the Psychology of Crime

Although criminal profiling is mainly associated with modern forensics, its roots go back to the 19th century when investigators first tried to apply psychology to crime investigations. However, significant development in this field came in the 20th century, largely thanks to the FBI's efforts and pioneering work by profilers who transformed criminal behavior analysis into a scientific methodology.

The Beginnings of Profiling: Jack the Ripper

One of the earliest attempts at profiling dates to the late 19th century, when London police sought to capture Jack the Ripper, one of the most infamous serial killers in history. Investigators analyzed the brutal murders in London's Whitechapel district, attempting to construct a psychological portrait of the killer. Forensic doctor Thomas Bond created one of the first unofficial profiles, describing the Ripper as a solitary person with possible personality disorders. Though Jack the Ripper was never caught, the case inspired future generations of investigators to combine psychology with criminal investigations.

The FBI and the Birth of Modern Profiling

Criminal profiling gained prominence in the 1970s when the FBI established a specialized unit focused on serial murders and sexual crimes. Profilers like John E. Douglas and Robert Ressler began systematically analyzing serial killers. They conducted interviews with incarcerated killers such as Ted Bundy, Edmund Kemper, and David Berkowitz (the "Son of Sam") to gain insights into their motives and behavioral patterns.

In 1978, the FBI founded the Behavioral Science Unit (BSU), which specialized in analyzing criminal behavior. This unit created psychological profiles for criminals and assisted in complex investigations. John Douglas, one of the BSU's leading figures, played a key role in defining the foundations of contemporary profiling. His work, chronicled in books like *Mindhunter*, marked a significant milestone in the evolution of profiling.

The Psychology of Crime

The development of profiling was also shaped by the psychology of crime, which studies the mechanisms, motivations, and emotions behind offenders' actions. Psychologists like David Canter in the UK developed theories on the spatial and emotional behavior of criminals. They examined how the crime scene's location and the offender's behavior at the scene could indicate psychological profiles and thought processes.

Profiling is more than crime analysis—it's an attempt to understand the motives behind violence. Does the killer act impulsively, out of passion, or through long-term planning? Does the offender have psychological disorders, or are they fully aware of their actions? Answers to these questions help investigators narrow down suspects and anticipate how an offender might act in the future.

Groundbreaking Profiling Cases

One of the most notable cases where profiling played a key role was that of the Unabomber, Theodore Kaczynski. For years, Kaczynski sent bombs to various institutions across the United States, killing and injuring many. Psychological profiling helped investigators realize that the Unabomber was likely a reclusive individual with an academic background, eventually leading to his capture.

Another prominent case was the BTK Killer—Dennis Rader, who murdered in Kansas during the 1970s and 80s. Rader eluded capture for years, but profiling, along with analysis of letters he sent to the press, ultimately led to his arrest in 2005.

Today, profiling continues to be an essential tool in modern investigations, combining insights from psychology and criminology to deepen our understanding of criminal minds and behavior.

How a Serial Killer Profile is Created

Creating a profile for a serial killer is a complex process that combines physical evidence analysis with a psychological evaluation of the offender's behavior. Profilers seek to understand the traits, motivations, and behavioral patterns that characterize the criminal, helping to predict future actions and narrow down the suspect pool. This process involves analyzing crime scenes, victim behavior, and the psychological and emotional aspects of the offender.

Step 1: Crime Scene Analysis

The first step in profiling is a thorough examination of the crime scene, where investigators gather evidence and try to reconstruct the events. Understanding whether the crime was planned and precise or impulsive and chaotic is essential. Organized offenders often leave fewer traces and act methodically, whereas disorganized offenders may leave numerous clues, such as fingerprints or blood.

Investigators also examine how the offender treated the victim: Was there evidence of torture or a quick death? Was the body hidden or left on display? Such details help in identifying psychological traits, such as a need for control, rage, or a desire to demonstrate dominance over the victim.

Step 2: Pattern Analysis

Serial killers often operate according to a specific pattern that profilers try to identify. This analysis covers how the offender chooses victims, how they interact with them, and how they carry out the crime. For instance, Ted Bundy selected young, attractive women with similar appearances, suggesting they may have resembled someone he harbored resentment towards.

Profilers also pay attention to the offender's modus operandi (method of committing the crime) and any "signature" left behind—a personal element unique to the offender. This could be distinct injuries inflicted on the victim or letters sent to the media, as seen with the Zodiac Killer. Unlike the modus operandi, the signature rarely changes, even if the offender adapts their methods.

Step 3: Psychological Assessment

With evidence gathered and behavioral patterns identified, profilers create a psychological portrait of the offender. Combining criminal analysis with psychology, they seek to define the type of person the offender might be, considering factors like intelligence level, emotional stability, potential mental disorders, and life history.

Psychological profiles may include possible childhood traumas, sadistic tendencies, or needs fulfilled by committing the crime, such as control, revenge, or recognition. Profiler assessments also explore whether the offender might be introverted and reclusive or extroverted and attention-seeking. They might also assess any specialized knowledge, such as medical skills (as speculated with Jack the Ripper) or impulsive, chaotic behavior.

Step 4: Creating the Profile

Based on the collected data, profilers develop a detailed report that includes the offender's likely appearance, age, social background, education, occupation, and possible residence. The profile may also provide predictions about the offender's future actions—where they may strike next and factors influencing their decisions.

The profile includes recommendations for investigators, such as which suspects to interview and what clues might aid in identifying the offender. Although profiling doesn't provide absolute answers, it helps narrow the search and understand the offender's psychological motives, increasing the likelihood of capture.

Profiling in Action: The Zodiac Case

In the Zodiac Killer case, profilers created a psychological profile based on his letters to the press and his violent crimes. Analysis of his writing style and messages suggested he might be highly intelligent, possibly with cryptography or military knowledge. Although Zodiac was never identified, profiling was crucial in efforts to understand his motives and behavior.

Test Your Skills – Create Your Own Offender Profile

Criminal profiling is a fascinating but complex task that requires analyzing both physical and psychological evidence. Now it's your chance to test your skills by creating a profile. Based on the crime description below, try to create a profile of the offender. Consider motivations, methods, and possible appearance or behavior. You can compare your answers with the example profile provided at the end.

Crime Description:

In a small town in the northern part of the country, a series of brutal attacks on women aged 25 to 40 have occurred. The women were alone in their homes at night when the attacks happened. The offender entered through windows or unlocked doors. All victims were beaten and strangled, but there were no signs of sexual assault or robbery. In several instances, odd arrangements were found at the scene, such as upright knives or covered mirrors.

Local authorities suspect this may be the work of a serial killer. The offender seems familiar with the area, as the attacks are spread within a small radius and take place in hard-to-access locations. These crimes have occurred over the past six months, with victims chosen seemingly at random, and without economic or sexual motives.

Guiding Questions for Creating the Profile:

Organized or Disorganized?
Did the offender act methodically, planning the attacks, or were these impulsive acts? What evidence suggests either approach?

Motivation
What might motivate the offender? Is there a desire to control victims, anger toward a certain type of person, or satisfaction derived from the violence itself?

Modus Operandi and Signature
What unique traits characterize this offender? Does the lack of sexual assault or robbery suggest anything? What might be the meaning behind the strange arrangements left at the crime scene?

Who Might the Offender Be?
Based on the behavior and actions, try to identify who the offender might be. Consider age, education, employment status, familiarity with the area, and potential living proximity.

Example Profile:

Organized Offender – The offender operates with forethought and precision. The selection of victims and entry methods indicate premeditation. He appears familiar with the neighborhood and navigates the area comfortably, suggesting he lives nearby or has a good knowledge of the town.

Motivation – The offender may be driven by deeply-rooted anger toward women. The absence of theft suggests that material gain is not a motive. The lack of sexual assault implies that the offender's satisfaction comes not from physical gratification but from exerting control and power over the victims.

Modus Operandi – Entering through windows or doors suggests that the offender is confident and skilled. The unusual object arrangements may indicate a "signature," hinting at potential psychological issues. The covered mirrors suggest that the offender might avoid looking at his own reflection—perhaps due to feelings of shame or identity issues.

Offender Profile – Likely a male in his 30s to 40s, single, struggling with social relationships. He probably lives in the vicinity, knows the area well, and may have a history of mental health issues or past violent behaviors, especially toward women. He operates at night, possibly indicating a flexible or unstable job, or lack of employment.

This example demonstrates how to create an offender profile based on limited information. Now that you understand the basics, try developing your own offender profile based on the described crime

6. Crime Scene Investigation

Conduct an Investigation: Fictional Crime Scene
Your task is to take on the role of detective and conduct an investigation based on a fictional crime scene. Careful analysis of the crime scene, traces of evidence, and the behavior of the offender will help you

uncover what happened. Gather the evidence and try to solve the mystery of this crime. Remember, even the smallest clue can be significant!

Crime Scene Description:

A fourth-floor apartment in a tenement building. The crime occurred at night, around 2:00 a.m. The victim, a 35-year-old woman, was found dead on the living room floor, lying face down near an overturned table. The window is open, with scattered books and documents around. The apartment's front door was locked, and the locks were undamaged.

No weapon was found at the crime scene. There are visible strangulation marks on the victim's neck, but no other injuries on her body. Police found no fingerprints or direct evidence indicating a break-in. A neighbor from the apartment across the hall reported hearing an argument a few hours earlier, but did not see anyone entering or leaving the apartment. On the table in the living room, there is an unfinished glass of wine and a pack of cigarettes.

Police suspect that the offender may have been known to the victim, as there are no signs of forced entry, and the door was locked from the inside. However, there are some ambiguities that require further investigation.

Investigation Questions:

- What could have been the weapon? – There is no weapon at the scene, but the marks on the victim's neck suggest strangulation. What might the offender have used?
- Are there any inconsistencies at the crime scene? – The scattered books and documents suggest a struggle, but the lack of other injuries could indicate other causes for the disorder. What else might raise suspicions?
- What does the open window signify? – Could the offender have escaped through the window? Or is it just a decoy meant to mislead investigators?
- What is the significance of the wine glass and cigarette pack? – Could they suggest that the victim had company before her death? Could these items be connected to the offender?
- What role might the neighbor who reported the argument play? – Are their statements credible? Could they have missed something? Is it possible the argument was related to the murder?

Your Investigation:

Try to answer the above questions by analyzing the available evidence and clues. Connect the facts, consider the offender's motivations, and try to create a possible crime scenario. Remember, every detail may be important!

Evidence Search: Identify Inconsistencies

- ### Crime Description:

In a luxury apartment, the body of a 45-year-old man was found. The victim was lying on the bed in the bedroom, with a firearm on the floor nearby. The man had a gunshot wound to the head, and the gun was found near his hand, suggesting suicide. A farewell note on the nightstand indicated that the victim may have been suffering from depression.

However, several details raised the investigators' suspicions. First, there was no gunpowder residue on the victim's hands, which is unusual in a firearm suicide case. Second, there were no fingerprints on the gun or the note. The apartment door was locked from the inside, and the windows were tightly closed. The victim's wife had been away but returned a few hours after the crime was discovered.

Police are puzzled—was this truly a suicide, or could someone have staged this crime?

- ### Inconsistencies to Identify:

Gunpowder Residue on the Victim's Hands – The absence of gunpowder residue is a major inconsistency. If the man had indeed committed suicide, there should be gunpowder on his hands from firing the weapon. What does this imply?

No Fingerprints on the Gun – A suicide victim holding a gun would typically leave fingerprints on it. The lack of fingerprints might suggest that someone else held the gun and wiped it clean afterward.

Farewell Note – Was the note written by the victim, or could it have been forged? The absence of fingerprints on the note raises suspicion. It's also worth asking if the handwriting matches the victim's style.

Locked Doors and Windows – The door being locked from the inside suggests the perpetrator knew how to mislead investigators. Is it possible that someone could have exited the apartment and locked the door in an unconventional way (e.g., using specialized tools)?

The Wife's Alibi – Was the victim's wife truly away? Or was her return shortly after the body was discovered a coincidence? Could her trip have been a pretext to stage the suicide?

- ## Your Task:

Your task is to identify which of these inconsistencies might indicate that this was a murder rather than a suicide. Consider every detail—the absence of gunpowder, fingerprints, the alibi—and think about what the true events might have been. Was the crime carefully staged to look like a suicide, or could there be a hidden emotional motive?

Conduct an Investigation: Mysterious Murder on the Beach

As the detective, your task is to solve the mystery surrounding a murder that took place on a beach in a small coastal town. You have access to evidence descriptions, witness accounts, and several key facts that may help you unravel the case. Can you determine what really happened?

Crime Scene Description:

The victim, a 42-year-old man, was found dead at dawn on the beach. His body was located near the water's edge, close to large rocks, lying on his back. He was dressed in everyday clothing—a shirt and jeans—and documents were found in his wallet. The victim was also holding a small, unopened bottle of water in his hand. There were no visible injuries, but there was some sand on his face, suggesting he may have been pressed to the ground.

Investigators determined that footprints from both the victim and a second person were present on the beach, with the second individual approaching the victim from the direction of the sea. Two different shoe sizes suggest that this person might have been significantly lighter. No weapon or other tools were found near the scene. However, a set of car keys was discovered about ten meters away, close to a vehicle parked near the beach.

The only witness was a woman walking her dog, who saw the man talking with someone in the dark around 4:00 a.m. She only observed their silhouettes from a distance and could not identify the other person. About half an hour later, her dog began acting agitated, drawing her attention. Shortly after, she stumbled upon the man's body.

Investigative Questions:

What significance could the unopened bottle in the victim's hand have? – Could it have been used in the crime, or does it point to an unexpected turn of events?

What do the footprints in the sand reveal? – The footprints suggest the victim was in the company of another person. Could the approach from the sea indicate an unexpected attack?

What might be the cause of death with no visible injuries? – Could he have been strangled, poisoned, or died from natural causes? What points to foul play?

What role do the car keys play? – Do they belong to the victim, or possibly the perpetrator? Were the keys accidentally dropped or intentionally left?

What is the significance of the witness's account? – Could someone else have been nearby and seen more than the witness realized? What might the dog's strange behavior indicate?

Your Investigation:

Based on the available information, try to answer the questions and develop your own theory about what might have happened. Pay attention to small details that may reveal the true course of events—for example, the significance of the water bottle, the footprints in the sand, and the dog's mysterious behavior.

Famous Crime Scenes and How They Were Investigated

Crime scenes often become iconic in forensic history when the crimes committed there attract massive media and public attention. Analyzing every detail of a crime scene is crucial to understanding the events and identifying the perpetrator. In this section, we will examine a few famous crime scenes and how they were investigated, leading to the discovery of key evidence.

The Murder of Nicole Brown Simpson and Ron Goldman

Crime Scene: Nicole Brown Simpson's home in Los Angeles, June 12, 1994.

In this case, careful examination of the crime scene was vital, as both Nicole Brown Simpson and her friend Ron Goldman were brutally murdered with a knife. Blood traces were found leading away from the victims' bodies, along with a bloody glove and shoe prints.

Key Elements of the Crime Scene Investigation:

Shoe Prints: Footprints found at the crime scene were later linked to Bruno Magli shoes, becoming a crucial piece of evidence.

DNA Analysis: Blood analysis at the scene matched O.J. Simpson's DNA, although the defense challenged this evidence, alleging evidence tampering.

The Glove: The bloody glove became symbolic of the case, especially after Simpson attempted to put it on during the trial, with the defense arguing, "If it doesn't fit, you must acquit."

This crime scene became one of the most thoroughly examined in history, highlighting the importance of properly securing evidence for investigation.

Jeffrey Dahmer's Apartment

Crime Scene: The Milwaukee apartment of serial killer Jeffrey Dahmer, where he murdered 17 young men between 1978 and 1991.

When police entered Dahmer's apartment in July 1991, they discovered horrific evidence of his crimes. The crime scene was a key piece of evidence, shocking investigators with Dahmer's brutality and his meticulous storage of his victims' body parts.

Key Elements of the Crime Scene Investigation:

Victims' Body Parts: Dismembered bodies were found stored in his freezer and barrels of acid. Investigators used this evidence to reconstruct what had happened to the victims.

Photos of Victims: Dahmer had taken photographs of his victims at different stages, which became crucial evidence of his guilt.

Chemical Traces: Chemicals used to dissolve bodies and dismembering tools were found in the apartment, unequivocally pointing to his actions.

Dahmer's crime scene was undeniable evidence of his sadistic practices, with every small clue analyzed by experts.

The Sharon Tate Murders (Manson Family)

Crime Scene: Residence on Cielo Drive in Beverly Hills, August 8-9, 1969.

The murder of Sharon Tate and her guests at her Beverly Hills home was one of the most brutal and shocking events in crime history. Charles Manson's followers broke into the house and murdered everyone inside, including the pregnant Sharon Tate.

Key Elements of the Crime Scene Investigation:

Blood Writings: Manson's followers wrote the word "PIG" in the victim's blood on the door, a distinct element of their crimes that investigators linked to other Manson killings.

Method of Injury: Forensic examination showed the victims were brutally stabbed, and precise analysis of the wounds helped investigators reconstruct the events.

Scattered Bodies: The victims' bodies were found in various places within the residence, suggesting they attempted to escape the attackers. Analysis of these signs helped create a profile of the killers.

The crime scene was examined for days, and the sheer brutality of the murders attracted massive media attention.

Assassination of John F. Kennedy

Crime Scene: Dealey Plaza, Dallas, November 22, 1963.

The assassination of U.S. President John F. Kennedy is one of the most studied and controversial cases in history. The President was shot while traveling in a motorcade in Dallas, and the investigation into his death has continued for decades.

Key Elements of the Crime Scene Investigation:

Bullet Trajectories: Investigators meticulously analyzed the bullet trajectories to determine where the shots originated, focusing most on the window of the book depository where Lee Harvey Oswald fired.

Driver and Security Behavior: Footage and photographs provided numerous clues about the progression of the attack and the delayed response of security personnel.

Weapon Analysis: The rifle used to fire the shots was thoroughly examined, with ballistic analysis serving as key evidence in the investigation.

JFK's assassination remains one of the most analyzed crimes in history, with Dealey Plaza continuing to stir up controversy.

The Hinterkaifeck Farm Murders

Crime Scene: A remote farm in Hinterkaifeck, Germany, March 31, 1922.

One of the most mysterious and unsolved crimes occurred at Hinterkaifeck farm, where six people—the family members and their maid—were brutally murdered with a pickaxe. Despite extensive investigation, the crime remains unsolved to this day.

Key Elements of the Crime Scene Investigation:

Body Positions: The victims were found in various locations on the farm, and their placement suggested that the killer may have lured them into the barn one by one.

Footprints in the Snow: Despite snow covering the area, no footprints led away from the farm, suggesting the perpetrator may have stayed there for days.

Strange Sounds and Traces: Before the murders, family members reported hearing strange noises and finding unfamiliar footprints in the snow leading to the house, hinting that the perpetrator might have been watching them for some time.

Despite thorough investigations, the Hinterkaifeck murders remain a mystery, and the crime scene still instills fear.

All of these crime scenes demonstrate the importance of careful analysis of clues and evidence. Each detail can bring investigators closer to discovering the truth and capturing the perpetrator.

7. Famous Detectives and Investigations

- The World of Iconic Detectives: Sherlock Holmes and Others

Detectives have long fascinated readers and audiences around the world. Thanks to their intelligence, analytical skills, and unconventional thinking, they've become heroes of numerous books, films, and TV series. The world of literature and film is rich with both fictional and real-life detectives whose work has inspired generations. This section highlights some of the most renowned detectives, both fictional and real.

- ### Sherlock Holmes – The Archetypal Detective

Sherlock Holmes, created by Sir Arthur Conan Doyle, is undoubtedly the most famous detective in literary history. First appearing in A Study in Scarlet in 1887, Holmes quickly became a pop culture icon. He is known for his deductive abilities, his keen eye for detail, and his unconventional approach to solving mysteries.

One of Holmes' primary tools was logical reasoning—the ability to draw conclusions from seemingly insignificant details. He could read a person's entire life story by analyzing something as minor as footprints or cigarette ash. In Holmes' world, there was no such thing as a coincidence; every clue, no matter how small, led him closer to the truth.

However, Holmes never worked alone. Dr. John Watson, his companion and narrator in most of the stories, also played the role of loyal friend and support in solving even the most challenging cases. Watson represented the reader, often astonished by Holmes' abilities, adding an additional dimension to the stories.

- ### Hercule Poirot – Agatha Christie's Master of Deduction

Hercule Poirot, a character created by Agatha Christie, is another legendary detective known worldwide. Poirot, a Belgian detective with impeccable manners and exceptional intelligence, solved even the toughest criminal cases using his "little gray cells." His methods differed from Holmes'—Poirot focused on the psychology of the crime, analyzing motives and human behavior rather than just physical evidence.

His most famous cases, such as Murder on the Orient Express and Death on the Nile, are classics of crime literature. Always elegant, with meticulously groomed mustaches, Poirot solved cases in ways that seemed almost magical, yet were always logical. His ability to discern the smallest nuances in human behavior made him an unmatched detective.

- ## Philip Marlowe – The Hardboiled Noir Detective

Philip Marlowe, created by Raymond Chandler, is a very different type of detective from Holmes or Poirot. Operating in the dark, gritty world of 1940s and 1950s Los Angeles, Marlowe is the hero of numerous noir novels, such as The Big Sleep and Farewell, My Lovely. His detective work involves not only logical reasoning but also confronting corruption, crime, and moral ambiguity.

Though tough and cynical, Marlowe holds a deeply ingrained sense of justice. He doesn't work for fame or money but because he believes in bringing order to a world marred by lawlessness. Unlike Holmes or Poirot, Marlowe often faces physical danger, yet his intelligence and determination always lead him to solve the case.

- ## Columbo – The Detective in a Trench Coat

Columbo, portrayed by Peter Falk, is the protagonist of one of the most popular detective series. At first glance, Columbo may appear as an unassuming, disheveled inspector in an old coat, but his intellect and persistence make him an outstanding investigator. His approach differs from classic detectives—Columbo usually knows the culprit from the start, but instead of focusing on solving a mystery, he works to gather proof of guilt.

What makes Columbo unique is his investigative style—seemingly scattered, always asking "random" and "annoying" questions, he ultimately uncovers the truth. His friendly, chaotic manner often misled criminals, who didn't realize how clever an opponent they faced.

- ## Real Detectives: Allan Pinkerton and Vidocq

We can't forget the real detectives who revolutionized the world of criminal investigation. Allan Pinkerton, founder of the famous Pinkerton National Detective Agency, was a pioneer in modern investigation. His agency became renowned for solving complex cases, including foiling an assassination attempt on President Abraham Lincoln.

Another legendary detective was Eugène François Vidocq, who in the 19th century established the world's first professional detective agency and became a model for many fictional detectives. A former criminal himself, Vidocq became an expert at catching criminals and introduced many innovative investigative techniques, such as the use of fingerprints and undercover infiltration.

Sherlock Holmes and Reality: Fact vs. Fiction

Sherlock Holmes, created by Sir Arthur Conan Doyle, became a literary icon and the embodiment of the ideal detective. Although his deductive and analytical skills seem extraordinary, many of the methods he employed in his adventures were rooted in real-life forensic techniques. In this section, we explore which elements of Sherlock Holmes' stories were inspired by actual investigative methods and which belong to the realm of fiction.

- Deduction and Detail Analysis

Sherlock Holmes: Holmes' greatest strength lay in his ability to draw conclusions from seemingly insignificant details. He could deduce a person's profession by analyzing footprints, clothing, or even cigarette ash. Deduction was his primary tool for solving mysteries.

Reality: Deduction is indeed a real investigative technique, though often exaggerated in literature. Detectives analyze evidence like shoe prints, fingerprints, and blood traces to reconstruct events. However, Holmes' ability to read a person's entire life from a single detail is more literary hyperbole than real detective work. In reality, deduction is a process of gradual evidence gathering, rather than instant conclusions.

- Fingerprint Analysis (Dactyloscopy)

Sherlock Holmes: In the stories, Holmes frequently analyzes fingerprints as crucial evidence, notably in The Adventure of the Abbey Grange.

Reality: Fingerprint analysis, known as dactyloscopy, was an actual innovation during Conan Doyle's time. Though Holmes seemed to master this technique, its widespread application only began in the late 1890s, soon after the first Holmes stories were published. In 1892, Sir Francis Galton developed a fingerprint classification system, making fingerprint analysis one of the cornerstones of forensic science.

- ## Chemistry and Laboratory Testing

Sherlock Holmes: In many stories, Holmes uses his own laboratory to analyze chemical substances, such as poisons or trace residues. In The Sign of Four, he employs chemical analysis to help uncover the background of the case.

Reality: Conan Doyle drew on actual scientific knowledge. By the late 19th century, chemical analysis was becoming vital in forensics, especially for detecting poisons and toxins. In reality, detectives relied on laboratory tests to identify trace substances at crime scenes, making Holmes a precursor of what has since become standard in forensic labs.

- ## Footprint and Shoe Print Analysis

Sherlock Holmes: Holmes often examines footprints at crime scenes, drawing detailed conclusions from them. For example, in A Study in Scarlet, Holmes examines footprints to determine who was at the crime scene and what their motives might have been.

Reality: Shoe print analysis has indeed been, and still is, a key part of forensic work. Footprints can reveal shoe size, height, weight, and even a person's gait. While footprint analysis was not as advanced in the 19th century, the technique has since become more precise, and investigators today can use technology to identify specific brands and types of shoes.

- ## Psychological Profiling

Sherlock Holmes: Although Holmes did not use this term, he performed psychological analysis on criminals in many stories. In The Adventure of the Empty House, he analyzes a criminal's behavior to predict their next move.

Reality: Criminal profiling only gained prominence in the 20th century, primarily through the FBI's work in the 1970s and 1980s. Psychological profiling became a valuable tool for understanding criminal motivations and predicting future actions. While Holmes used intuitive techniques akin to profiling, the scientific foundation for this method emerged much later.

- Inductive vs. Deductive Reasoning

Sherlock Holmes: Holmes often referenced his "deductive" method of reasoning. However, most of his conclusions were based on induction—drawing general conclusions from specific observations.

Reality: Deduction traditionally involves deriving specific conclusions from general principles, while induction is the process of moving from specific observations to broader generalizations. Holmes' methods, though often termed deductive, were actually closer to inductive reasoning—he observed specific traces and then formed general conclusions about the perpetrator.

- Trailing Criminals and Disguises

Sherlock Holmes: Holmes often trailed criminals by disguising himself and concealing his identity. He used various disguises to avoid recognition by enemies, making it a staple part of his investigations.

Reality: Disguises and undercover methods were commonly used by detectives, especially in the 19th century. Eugène François Vidocq, a French detective and former criminal, was known for frequently changing his appearance to infiltrate criminal circles. Holmes likely drew inspiration from figures like Vidocq, and his use of disguises reflects real techniques employed by investigators.

- Fact or Fiction?

Sherlock Holmes remains a legendary detective whose methods in many ways anticipated reality. His (inductive rather than deductive) methodology, knowledge of chemistry, shoe print analysis, and keen observation were inspired by real forensic techniques, though they were in their early stages during Conan Doyle's era. The character of Holmes significantly impacted the development of forensic science, inspiring real-life detectives to refine and improve their investigative methods.

What Does the Work of Modern Detectives Look Like?

Modern detective work is vastly different from the portrayals we know from literature and film. Although many techniques popularized by fictional detectives like Sherlock Holmes are reflected in today's investigations, modern detectives use advanced technology, analytical tools, and scientific support to solve complex cases. This section explores the day-to-day work of contemporary detectives and the challenges they face.

- Modern Technology: DNA, Data Analysis, and Digital Traces

One of the most significant changes in modern detective work is access to advanced technology. DNA analysis has become a crucial tool in forensic science, allowing investigators to identify suspects from minimal biological traces, like hair, blood, saliva, or skin cells. Even a small amount of DNA can solve decades-old cases, as seen in "cold cases" that are now being revisited thanks to modern technology.

The digital age has also introduced the necessity of analyzing data from electronic devices. Investigators examine cell phones, computers, surveillance footage, and even social media activity. Digital traces—like internet search histories, GPS locations, and conversation logs—are invaluable sources of information.

- Collecting Evidence at Crime Scenes

While digital technologies play a huge role, the foundation of detective work still lies in meticulous crime scene analysis. This is where physical evidence, such as fingerprints, footprints, material fibers, bloodstains, or weapons, is collected. Advanced techniques, like using UV light, lasers, or magnetic powders for fingerprint analysis, reveal traces invisible to the naked eye.

Securing a crime scene is crucial to an investigation. Any minor error in this process—like improper handling of evidence or unauthorized people entering the scene—can ruin the potential for valuable information. Therefore, modern detectives work closely with forensic technicians who specialize in collecting and analyzing evidence.

- ### Profiling and Behavioral Analysis

Although criminal profiling has been popularized by books and TV shows like Mindhunter and Criminal Minds, contemporary profiling techniques are based on hard data and years of behavioral research. Detectives, using insights from criminal psychologists, develop profiles based on the perpetrator's methods, victim selection, and potential motivations.

Modern profilers analyze the "modus operandi" (method of operation) and "signature" (distinct, repetitive elements left at the crime scene). These techniques help narrow down suspects and can even predict future actions of the criminal, which is key in apprehending them.

- ### Teamwork and Collaboration with Other Agencies

Contemporary investigations are highly collaborative. Unlike the solitary detectives of literature, today's detectives work in teams that include other investigators, forensic technicians, forensic scientists, psychologists, and lawyers. Each team member brings specialized knowledge, increasing the chances of solving the case.

Additionally, detectives often work alongside agencies like the FBI, Interpol, or local law enforcement. In international cases, such as organized crime or terrorism, collaboration is essential. Examples of such teamwork include cases related to human trafficking, drug rings, and cybercrime.

- ### Civil Investigations: Private Detectives

Not all detectives work for police or government agencies. The modern world also has private detectives who handle civil cases, like investigations into infidelity, financial fraud, missing persons, and corporate investigations. Private detectives often work for companies or individuals, requiring a high degree of discretion and analytical skills.

Although private investigators don't have the same authority as police detectives, they often work in parallel with law enforcement, providing valuable information that can assist in solving cases. They also use modern tools like surveillance, digital analysis, and wiretapping to gather evidence for their clients.

- ### New Challenges: Cybercrime and Digital Traces

One of the biggest challenges for modern detectives is the increasing prevalence of digital crimes. Cybercrime—including fraud, identity theft, hacking, and trafficking of drugs and weapons in the dark web—requires a new set of skills. Detectives need to be proficient in analyzing digital traces, tracking online activity, and securing data.

Many investigations now begin at the computer—analyzing emails, internet browsing history, and social media activity can provide valuable insights into a criminal's actions and plans. Examples include cases involving financial fraud, scams, and organized online crime.

- ### Ethical Challenges: Privacy Boundaries and Surveillance

Modern technology has given detectives unprecedented capabilities for tracking and monitoring suspects. However, these capabilities also bring ethical challenges. In an era of widely accessible surveillance technology, investigations must balance the need to solve cases with the protection of citizens' privacy.

Techniques like wiretapping, monitoring social media, and analyzing data from surveillance cameras and cell phones raise questions about where the right to privacy ends and public safety begins. Modern detectives must be mindful of these boundaries and operate within legal regulations to avoid infringing on civil rights, even if the objective is noble.

- ### Summary

The work of modern detectives combines traditional investigative methods with cutting-edge technology. While deduction, observation, and evidence analysis remain essential, technological advancements—from DNA analysis to cybercrime tracking—are changing the way investigations are conducted. Both police and private detectives must adapt to contemporary challenges to effectively solve cases in an increasingly complex world.

Real Investigations that Revolutionized Forensics

Over the years, several groundbreaking investigations have led to the development of new forensic techniques and investigative methods, forever changing the way cases are solved. Here are some of the most significant cases that transformed forensic science.

- The Ted Bundy Case: First Use of Computer Profiling

Ted Bundy, one of the most infamous serial killers, operated in the 1970s, murdering young women across multiple states in the U.S. Bundy's intelligence and charm made him a deceptive and dangerous figure who often escaped suspicion.

Key breakthroughs in Bundy's case:

Psychological Profiling: As Bundy committed his crimes, the FBI was developing psychological profiling techniques. His case became one of the first to attempt creating a serial killer profile based on behavioral analysis and modus operandi.

Use of Computers: In 1975, investigators used a computer system for the first time to connect information about victims and crime scenes across various states, leading them to identify Bundy as the main suspect.

Bundy's Escapes: Bundy's two escapes from custody underscored the need for stronger security in investigations and prison systems.

Bundy's case spurred the development of modern serial killer profiling techniques and the first use of computers for tracking information across jurisdictions.

- The Assassination of President John F. Kennedy: Ballistics and Bullet Trajectory Analysis

The assassination of John F. Kennedy on November 22, 1963, in Dallas, was one of the 20th century's most impactful events. The president's shooting at Dealey Plaza sparked not only enormous public emotion but also intense scrutiny of investigative methodologies.

How the JFK assassination advanced forensic science:

Ballistics Analysis: Investigators meticulously examined bullet trajectories to determine the origin of the shots. This analysis led to the theory that the shots were fired from the Texas School Book Depository, where Lee Harvey Oswald was located.

The Zapruder Film: An amateur film capturing the assassination became one of the most significant pieces of forensic evidence in history. Over the years, analyses of this footage were used to study bullet trajectories, security response times, and the president's movements.

Conspiracy Theories: While the JFK assassination remains controversial, ballistics, recreations, and video analysis have been instrumental in developing modern techniques for analyzing shootings and firearms use.

The JFK investigation initiated the development of advanced ballistics analysis and bullet trajectory reconstruction techniques.

The Golden State Killer Case: Breakthrough in DNA Usage

The Golden State Killer (Joseph James DeAngelo) terrorized California in the 1970s and 80s, committing a series of murders, assaults, and burglaries. He remained unidentified for decades until 2018, when he was identified through innovative use of DNA and genealogical databases.

Key elements of this investigation:

Genetic Genealogy Use: Investigators used crime scene DNA and compared it with public genealogy databases that contained DNA profiles of people searching for their ancestors. This led to a relative of DeAngelo, eventually resulting in his arrest.

Breakthrough in Investigative Techniques: The Golden State Killer case revolutionized how detectives could utilize DNA technology, opening new possibilities for solving cold cases.

Closure of a Long-Running Case: The case lasted over 40 years, and its resolution demonstrated how modern science could revolutionize forensics and catch criminals long after the crimes were committed.

The Oklahoma City Bombing: Development of Explosives Analysis Techniques

The 1995 bombing of the Alfred P. Murrah Federal Building in Oklahoma City by Timothy McVeigh was one of the deadliest acts of terrorism in U.S. history. McVeigh detonated a truck filled with explosives, killing 168 people and injuring hundreds.

Key aspects of this investigation:

Explosives Analysis: Investigators had to reconstruct the type and chemical composition of the explosive device to identify the perpetrator. Chemical analysis of explosive residue became crucial in identifying McVeigh.

Video Surveillance Analysis: Surveillance cameras captured McVeigh, allowing investigators to identify the vehicle he used and track his movements. Video analysis was key in connecting McVeigh to the bomb-laden truck.

Securing the Crime Scene: This investigation required innovative methods to secure the scene where evidence had been scattered or destroyed by the powerful explosion.

The Oklahoma City bombing investigation led to advances in explosives analysis techniques and greater emphasis on monitoring vehicles carrying dangerous materials.

The Lindbergh Case: Significance of Physical Evidence and Handwriting Analysis

The kidnapping and murder of famed aviator Charles Lindbergh's son in 1932 was one of the most publicized and shocking cases of the time. The ransom demands and the child's tragic death captivated national attention.

Key elements of the investigation:

Physical Evidence: Investigators linked the wooden ladder used to access the Lindbergh home with the workshop of the suspect, Bruno Richard Hauptmann.

Handwriting Analysis: The ransom note was handwritten, and experts compared the handwriting with samples from Hauptmann, which was critical in the prosecution.

Tracking Techniques: The analysis of evidence and the movements of the suspects led to Hauptmann's arrest.

This case was pivotal in establishing the importance of handwriting analysis and physical evidence, setting standards still used in forensic science today.

Each of these cases played a crucial role in developing modern forensic techniques that forever changed the way investigations are conducted. From DNA analysis to ballistics to explosives study, these real-life investigations revolutionized forensic science and set new standards for detective work worldwide.

8. Notorious Trials: The Case of O.J. Simpson

- The Trial of O.J. Simpson: Where Lies the Truth?

The trial of O.J. Simpson, renowned athlete and celebrity, remains one of the most media-covered and controversial court cases in U.S. history. It began in 1994 following the brutal murder of his ex-wife, Nicole Brown

Simpson, and her friend, Ron Goldman. This case captured global attention, and its conclusion – Simpson's acquittal – sparked countless protests, discussions, and conspiracy theories. To this day, the question remains: where does the truth lie?

- The Crime and Circumstances

Nicole Brown Simpson and Ron Goldman were brutally murdered outside Nicole's home on June 12, 1994. Their bodies were found with multiple stab wounds, indicative of a vicious attack. Investigators quickly focused on O.J. Simpson, who had a turbulent relationship with his ex-wife. Reports of domestic violence in their marriage further directed the police's attention to Simpson as the prime suspect.

A pivotal moment came when Simpson, instead of appearing for questioning, fled in a now-infamous white Ford Bronco, leading to a dramatic televised chase.

- Evidence and Controversies

Simpson's trial hinged on various pieces of evidence, many of which became hotly contested.

DNA Analysis: DNA evidence suggested that Simpson's blood was found at the crime scene, as well as a blood-stained glove linked to the murders. However, the defense contested this evidence, arguing it could have been tampered with by investigators. DNA testing was still relatively new and not fully accepted by the public as a reliable tool at the time.

The Famous Glove: A defining moment of the trial occurred when Simpson was asked to try on a blood-stained glove presented as evidence. The glove appeared too small, and Simpson's defense used this to argue he couldn't be the killer. Defense attorney Johnnie Cochran's iconic line, "If it doesn't fit, you must acquit," remains etched in public memory.

Police and Allegations of Racism: A significant part of the defense's argument focused on alleged racial motives within the LAPD. Detective Mark Fuhrman, who found key evidence, was accused of racism, with the defense suggesting he might have planted evidence to frame Simpson. Fuhrman, known to have used racist slurs, became central to undermining the integrity of the entire investigation.

- ## The Role of Media

The Simpson trial was broadcast live, turning it into a media spectacle. Millions worldwide followed every courtroom detail, and the case split public opinion. For many, the trial highlighted deep racial divides in the U.S.—many white viewers believed in Simpson's guilt, while many Black Americans saw him as a victim of racial prejudice and a flawed justice system.

The media played a critical role in shaping public perceptions of the case, often influencing how evidence and witness testimony were interpreted. Constant courtroom broadcasts turned the trial into a spectacle, where legal details were often overshadowed by personal dramas and sensationalized headlines.

- ## Acquittal and Aftermath

In October 1995, O.J. Simpson was acquitted of murder charges, a verdict that sparked widespread controversy and societal division. Some felt Simpson evaded justice due to his fame and wealth, which enabled him to afford top-notch defense attorneys. Others felt the justice system had worked properly and that the evidence against Simpson was inconclusive.

After his acquittal, Simpson faced a civil lawsuit filed by the victims' families. He was found liable for the deaths of Nicole Brown Simpson and Ron Goldman and ordered to pay substantial damages, further complicating his post-trial life.

Where Lies the Truth?

To this day, the O.J. Simpson trial raises lingering questions. Did Simpson truly murder his ex-wife and her friend, with the case manipulated by the defense? Or was he a victim of a corrupt system and racial bias? The Simpson case permanently altered the American justice system, yet the answer to "where does the truth lie?" remains ambiguous.

The O.J. Simpson trial stands as one of the most complex and divisive investigations in history, forcing society to examine the influence of media, the role of race, and how law and money can impact courtroom outcomes.

The O.J. Simpson Trial: Where Does the Truth Lie?

The trial of O.J. Simpson, famous athlete and celebrity, remains one of the most widely covered and controversial court cases in U.S. history. It began in 1994 following the brutal murder of his ex-wife, Nicole Brown Simpson, and her friend, Ron Goldman. The case captured global attention, and the trial's conclusion—Simpson's acquittal—sparked protests, debate, and conspiracy theories. To this day, the question remains: where does the truth lie?

- ### The Crime and Circumstances

Nicole Brown Simpson and Ron Goldman were brutally murdered outside Nicole's home on June 12, 1994. Their bodies were found with multiple stab wounds, indicating an extremely violent attack. Investigators quickly focused on O.J. Simpson, who had a turbulent relationship with his ex-wife. Their marriage had previously involved reports of domestic violence, which further heightened police suspicion toward Simpson as the primary suspect.

One of the most unforgettable moments occurred when Simpson failed to appear for questioning and instead fled in the now-iconic white Ford Bronco, leading to a live, dramatic televised chase.

- ### Evidence and Controversies

Simpson's trial centered on various pieces of evidence, many of which became the subject of intense debate and controversy.

DNA Analysis: One of the most critical pieces of evidence was the DNA analysis, which indicated that Simpson's blood was present at the crime scene. A glove covered in the victims' blood was also found, linking

Simpson to the murders. However, the defense contested these findings, suggesting that the evidence may have been manipulated by investigators. At the time, DNA testing had not yet gained full acceptance as a reliable tool in the public's eyes.

The Famous Glove: A turning point in the trial occurred when Simpson was asked to try on a blood-stained glove presented as evidence. In the courtroom, the glove appeared too small, and the defense used this to argue that Simpson could not have been the perpetrator. Defense attorney Johnnie Cochran's famous line, "If it doesn't fit, you must acquit," resonated with millions watching the trial.

Police and Racism Allegations: A significant element of the defense's case involved accusing the police of racially biased motives. Detective Mark Fuhrman, who discovered key evidence, was accused of racism, and the defense argued that the evidence might have been fabricated to frame Simpson. Fuhrman, who had a history of using racial slurs, became a focal point in challenging the investigation's credibility.

- ## The Role of the Media

The O.J. Simpson trial was broadcast live on television, making it a media spectacle. Millions worldwide followed the courtroom developments, and the case sharply divided public opinion. For many, the trial symbolized deep racial divides in the United States—white viewers often believed Simpson was guilty, while many African Americans saw him as a victim of racial prejudice and a biased legal system.

The media played a key role in shaping public perception of the trial and in influencing how evidence and witness testimony were viewed. Continuous courtroom coverage transformed the trial into a spectacle, where legal details were often overshadowed by personal drama and sensational headlines.

- ## Acquittal and Aftermath

In October 1995, O.J. Simpson was acquitted of murder charges, a verdict that generated considerable controversy and societal division. Many felt that Simpson evaded justice due to his fame and wealth, which allowed him to hire top defense lawyers. On the other hand, proponents of the acquittal argued that the justice system had worked properly and that the evidence against Simpson was insufficient.

Following the trial, the victims' families filed a civil suit against Simpson. In the civil court, he was found responsible for the deaths of Nicole Brown Simpson and Ron Goldman and was ordered to pay significant damages, adding further complications to his life after the trial.

- Where Does the Truth Lie?

To this day, the O.J. Simpson trial raises lingering questions. Did Simpson truly murder his ex-wife and her friend, with the defense manipulating the case? Or was he a victim of a corrupt system and racial bias? Simpson's case forever altered the American justice system, but the answer to "where does the truth lie?" remains inconclusive.

The O.J. Simpson trial stands as one of the most complex and divisive investigations in history, forcing society to examine the role of media, racial prejudice, and the extent to which law and wealth can influence courtroom outcomes.

The Amanda Knox Case: How the Media Influenced the Trial

The Amanda Knox case stands as one of the most widely covered and controversial trials of recent decades. In 2007, Knox, a young American, was accused of the brutal murder of her roommate, Meredith Kercher, in Perugia, Italy. For years, Knox's trial captivated global media, with the press's impact on public perception and the trial's proceedings becoming a significant topic of analysis. Ultimately, after years of appeals and varied verdicts, Knox was acquitted in 2015, but the question of how the media influenced the course of her trial remains crucial.

- ### The Perugia Crime: What Happened?

In November 2007, the body of Meredith Kercher, a British exchange student, was found in her rented apartment in Perugia, Italy. She had been strangled and fatally stabbed. Amanda Knox, her American roommate, and Knox's Italian boyfriend, Raffaele Sollecito, quickly became the prime suspects.

Police alleged that the murder resulted from a sexual encounter gone wrong, with Knox and Sollecito implicated. Another suspect, Rudy Guede, left fingerprints and DNA at the scene and was later convicted of the murder. However, both investigators and the media focused primarily on Knox and Sollecito.

- ### A Media Sensation: Amanda Knox as "Foxy Knoxy"

The media immediately seized on the story, turning Amanda Knox into the central figure of a media spectacle. Both Italian and international press began to paint Knox in a negative light, dubbing her "Foxy Knoxy"—a nickname suggesting cunning and seductive traits. This scandalous portrayal framed her as a sexually motivated instigator of the crime, a narrative that captivated media attention and made the trial an international sensation.

Tabloids sensationalized and exaggerated details of Knox's personal life, casting her less as a young student and more as a manipulative figure. Her behavior following the discovery of Meredith's body, such as displaying affection for Sollecito at the scene, was also interpreted negatively and depicted as evidence of her lack of remorse.

- ### Evidence and Controversies

Knox's trial was fraught with controversy over the evidence presented:

DNA Analysis: DNA traces from Knox were found on a knife that was alleged to be the murder weapon, though no traces from Kercher were detected. Additionally, Sollecito's DNA was found on Kercher's bra clasp. Defense attorneys argued that the evidence had been contaminated during the investigation. Later independent analysis showed the DNA evidence was unreliable due to procedural mistakes in collection and analysis.

Inconsistent Statements: Knox was repeatedly questioned by Italian police, and her statements changed several times. A critical moment was her initial admission that she was in the apartment during the murder, a statement she later retracted, claiming it was made under duress. This inconsistency complicated public perception of the case.

- ### The Media's Role in Shaping the Narrative

The media played an enormous role in Knox's trial, significantly influencing how she was viewed in Italy and worldwide. Especially in Italy, the press focused on sensational details from Knox's personal life, often downplaying or ignoring key evidence that might have challenged her guilt.

In the United States, the portrayal of Knox was more balanced. American media often depicted her as an innocent student caught in an unjust Italian legal system, while Italian media continued to present the "Foxy Knoxy" narrative, creating a divide in public perception across continents.

- ### Verdicts and Appeals: The Fight for Justice

In 2009, Amanda Knox and Raffaele Sollecito were convicted of murdering Meredith Kercher. Knox was sentenced to 26 years in prison, and Sollecito received 25 years. However, in 2011, after a series of appeals and re-examinations of the evidence, the court acquitted them, citing insufficient proof.

The media renewed its focus on the case, questioning how such a dramatic reversal could occur. Later, in 2013, the Italian Supreme Court overturned the acquittal and ordered another trial, leading to years of further appeals. Finally, in 2015, Italy's highest court definitively acquitted Amanda Knox and Sollecito, ending their prolonged legal ordeal.

- ### Media Influence on the Trial

The Amanda Knox case exemplifies the powerful impact the media can have on the course of a trial and on public perception of the accused. The press's role in shaping the narrative surrounding the case raised questions about journalistic ethics and the way media can manipulate public opinion. Throughout Knox's trial, the media not only reported events but actively crafted her public image, potentially influencing court decisions and shaping how the evidence was received by the public.

The media's involvement in Knox's portrayal contributed to the perception of her guilt long before any verdict was reached, a phenomenon often described as the "third estate" effect, where the press acts as an unofficial "judge" in the court of public opinion.

- Reflections: A Trial Under Media Pressure

The Amanda Knox trial revealed the dangers of excessive media exposure on a legal case. The media's influence can alter public perception of defendants, which in turn can affect trial outcomes. In Knox's case, the press did not merely cover the story but shaped her image in the eyes of millions worldwide.

In hindsight, the Knox case serves as a warning about the impact of media on judicial fairness, as well as a reflection on how easily evidence and behaviors of defendants can be manipulated in the public eye.

Trials That Changed Law and Society

Throughout history, certain trials have had significant impacts not only on the law but also on society as a whole. Some of these cases introduced changes to the justice system, while others sparked societal debates that reshaped perceptions of law and justice. In this section, we will explore a few key cases that revolutionized both the legal system and social life.

- ## The Case of Brown v. Board of Education (1954)

The Brown v. Board of Education decision by the U.S. Supreme Court is one of the most important rulings of the 20th century. Addressing racial segregation in public schools, this landmark ruling transformed the educational system and became a milestone in the American civil rights movement.

Case Background: In the 1950s, racial segregation was legal in many U.S. states under the doctrine of "separate but equal." In reality, schools for Black students were far less funded and equipped than those for white students.

Significance of the Ruling: In 1954, the U.S. Supreme Court unanimously ruled that racial segregation in public schools was unconstitutional, as it violated the 14th Amendment's guarantee of equal protection under the law. This groundbreaking decision ended legal racial segregation in American schools and initiated the movement toward equal rights for African Americans.

Social Impact: The Brown decision accelerated desegregation across the country, although the process took years in certain states. The case became a symbol of the fight against injustice and sparked social changes with lasting effects on civil rights in the United States.

- ## The Case of Roe v. Wade (1973)

The Roe v. Wade decision was one of the most controversial and significant U.S. Supreme Court rulings on women's right to abortion. The verdict sparked a nationwide debate on choice, reproductive rights, and morality, with consequences still felt today.

Case Background: Norma McCorvey, under the pseudonym "Jane Roe," filed a lawsuit against Texas, where abortion was illegal except to save the mother's life. McCorvey argued that the abortion ban violated her right to privacy.

Significance of the Ruling: In 1973, the Supreme Court ruled 7-2 that the right to abortion was part of the constitutional right to privacy protected by the 14th Amendment, making abortion legal across the country until the fetus became viable outside the womb (around the 24th week).

Social Impact: Roe v. Wade has sparked ongoing political and social debate, dividing American society between abortion rights supporters and opponents who have sought to overturn the decision. In 2022, the Supreme Court in Dobbs v. Jackson Women's Health Organization reversed Roe, re-igniting intense debate over abortion in the United States.

- The Nuremberg Trials (1945–1946)

The Nuremberg Trials were a series of international trials after World War II and the first in history to prosecute crimes against humanity, bringing Nazi leaders to justice. These trials not only revolutionized international law but also shaped the world's perspective on accountability for war crimes.

Case Background: Following the fall of Nazi Germany, the Allies decided to bring Nazi leaders responsible for war crimes, genocide, and crimes against humanity to trial. The main Nuremberg trial prosecuted 24 top Nazi officials, including Hermann Göring, Rudolf Hess, and Joachim von Ribbentrop.

Significance of the Verdict: The Nuremberg Trials introduced the concepts of "crimes against humanity" and "genocide" into international law. The judges ruled that even those acting on government orders could be held accountable for crimes contrary to international law. Most of the accused were sentenced to death or lengthy prison terms.

Social Impact: The Nuremberg Trials set a precedent for international courts and laid the foundation for modern international law, including the International Criminal Court. Nuremberg justice became a symbol that even the most powerful can be held accountable for their crimes.

The Miranda Case: Miranda v. Arizona (1966)

Miranda v. Arizona forever changed the rights of individuals detained by police in the United States. The ruling in this case introduced the requirement for police to inform suspects of their rights, now universally known as "Miranda rights."

Case Background: In 1963, Ernesto Miranda was arrested on charges of kidnapping and rape. During questioning, he confessed, but was not informed of his rights to remain silent or to have an attorney. Based on his confession, he was convicted, but his lawyers appealed, arguing that his constitutional rights had been violated.

Significance of the Ruling: The U.S. Supreme Court ruled that suspects must be informed of their rights before questioning. From this point on, police were required to recite the "Miranda rights," including the right to remain silent and the right to an attorney, with failure to do so potentially leading to evidence being dismissed.

Social Impact: The Miranda ruling significantly strengthened civil rights in the United States. Miranda rights became foundational to the modern justice system, ensuring that detainees are aware of their rights and can access legal defense.

The Dred Scott Case (1857): Law and Slavery

Dred Scott was an enslaved man who, in the 1850s, brought his case to court to seek recognition of his freedom. The Dred Scott v. Sandford decision resulted in one of the most controversial rulings in U.S. history, triggering outrage and contributing to the outbreak of the Civil War.

Case Background: Dred Scott, a slave, spent time in free territories and argued that this entitled him to freedom. His case reached the U.S. Supreme Court.

Significance of the Verdict: In 1857, the Supreme Court ruled that Scott had no right to sue because he was not a citizen but property. This decision also stated that Congress could not prohibit slavery in the territories, effectively reinforcing the institution of slavery.

Social Impact: The ruling sparked widespread outrage, deepening divisions between the North and South. It was one of the catalysts for the Civil War and ultimately the abolition of slavery. The Dred Scott case is often cited as an example of judicial injustice and extreme racial bias.

Each of these cases profoundly changed the justice system, impacting civil rights, individual protections, and social relations. They demonstrate how key court cases can shape society and introduce fundamental changes to legislation.

- 9. Life After Crime: Social and Psychological Consequences

Victims and Their Stories

Crimes, especially violent ones, leave a deep impact on the lives of victims, their families, and entire communities. Every victim's story is unique, yet trauma from experiencing violence or crime often becomes a defining element in life, affecting physical and emotional health as well as relationships with others. This section explores how victims' lives change after a crime and what challenges they frequently face.

- Life After Crime: The Struggle to Regain Normalcy

For many victims, returning to a "normal" life can be incredibly difficult. Surviving a crime often leads to a feeling of lost control over one's life and a shift in seeing the world as a safe place. Victims may feel threatened even in previously safe environments and often experience guilt, despite being the ones who suffered harm.

For instance, people who survive an assault may avoid places or situations that remind them of the traumatic event for a long time. These mechanisms are part of the psychological effects that can make daily functioning challenging.

- Isolation and a Sense of Alienation

Many crime victims feel isolated and alienated from society. They may struggle to form new relationships or return to work, school, or social life.

Fears of being judged or misunderstood can lead to feelings of loneliness.

For example, victims of sexual crimes often experience shame and fear of social judgment, which deepens their trauma. For young people, such experiences can affect their emotional and social development and self-perception.

- ## Long-Term Health Effects

Some crimes leave lasting physical impacts on victims' health. Physical injuries can lead to chronic pain, mobility issues, and the need for long-term rehabilitation. However, psychosomatic issues, such as insomnia, headaches, concentration difficulties, depression, or panic attacks, are more common as lasting effects of trauma.

Victims of assaults or wars, for instance, frequently suffer from anxiety disorders or post-traumatic stress disorder (PTSD). This condition can impact every aspect of life, from relationships with loved ones to career functionality.

- ## Stories of Well-Known Victims and Their Impact on Society

There are victims whose stories have led to legal changes or inspired broader social reflection on safety. Cases like that of Kitty Genovese, who was murdered while bystanders reportedly watched passively, sparked discussions about civic responsibility and the "bystander effect"—the tendency of witnesses to do nothing.

Another example is the story of Jaycee Dugard, who was held captive for 18 years by her abductor. Her story highlighted the need for improved procedures in missing persons cases and stricter oversight of sexual offenders.

- ## The Road to Justice: Hopes and Disappointments

For many crime victims, the judicial process represents a hope for justice and a means of healing and closing a painful chapter. However, the legal system can fall short of these expectations. Long waits, lack of convictions, or lenient sentences can leave victims feeling abandoned by the justice system.

For instance, when a perpetrator is released due to insufficient evidence, victims may feel that their suffering went unacknowledged. In such cases, psychologists and support from loved ones play a crucial role in helping victims cope emotionally and accept the legal realities.

Victims' stories highlight the importance of psychological support and adequate legal protection. As society becomes more aware of crime victims' issues, new strategies and programs are being developed to improve their lives after trauma.

How Crimes Transform Society

Every serious crime affects not only individuals but also society as a whole. Crimes, particularly those that are violent or of a large scale, often provoke strong emotions, fear, and reflection on safety, justice, and the value of human life. This section examines how crimes influence social structures and how they impact laws, justice systems, and public attitudes.

- ### Heightened Demand for Safety

In the wake of high-profile crimes, public feelings of insecurity often increase. People begin to worry more about their own safety and take measures to protect themselves and their families. This can lead to greater investment in security systems, such as surveillance cameras, alarms, or increased police presence on the streets.

For example, terrorist attacks in the 21st century have prompted heightened security measures at airports, shopping centers, and public spaces. Each incident results in strengthened procedures and regulations aimed at preventing future tragedies.

- ### Impact on Laws and the Justice System

High-profile crimes frequently lead to changes in legislation. Cases that shock the public may ignite debates about criminal penalties, legal processes, or the effectiveness of rehabilitation. In many instances, these changes aim to increase penalties, introduce new regulations, or improve victim protections.

For instance, the murder of Megan Kanka in the United States in 1994 led to the establishment of "Megan's Law," which requires sex offenders to register and makes this information publicly available. This measure has increased transparency about potential threats from some offenders in communities.

- Crime as a Catalyst for Social Change

Crimes that expose social inequalities, corruption, or flaws in the justice system can serve as catalysts for change. Society often responds to such cases by advocating reforms and pressing politicians to implement necessary changes. In these instances, crime acts as a "trigger" for widespread public debate, leading to reforms in civil rights, social equality, or minority protections.

For example, civil rights movements in the U.S. gained momentum following a series of police brutality cases, such as the death of George Floyd in 2020. This tragic event sparked global protests against racism and police violence, resulting in reforms aimed at increasing police transparency and combatting discrimination.

- Normalization of Surveillance and Monitoring

In response to rising crime and terrorism, many governments have increased citizen monitoring to prevent crime. The widespread presence of cameras, online activity tracking, and other forms of surveillance have become more common, impacting daily life and citizens' sense of privacy.

The United Kingdom, one of the most heavily monitored countries globally, has thousands of cameras surveilling public spaces. Following numerous terrorist attacks in Europe, many governments introduced new national security laws that limit citizens' privacy in the name of crime prevention.

- ## Impact on Social Relationships and Trust

In societies that experience high crime rates, trust between individuals often declines. Examples like rising fraud, cybercrime, and robberies can make people more suspicious of others and less willing to form new relationships. This phenomenon is particularly evident in cities with high crime rates, where residents feel a heightened fear of potential threats from strangers.

Reduced social trust can have far-reaching consequences, leading to isolation and lower social engagement. Society may become more closed, with people who were once eager to help others becoming more cautious and withdrawn.

- ## Popular Culture and Fascination with Crime

Crimes, especially shocking or unusual ones, often influence popular culture. Books, films, TV series, and documentaries about crimes capture society's attention, as people try to understand the motives of perpetrators and the workings of the justice system. This fascination has led to a growing interest in crime topics and the expansion of the "true crime" genre in popular culture.

However, this fascination can also have negative consequences—while it brings attention to crime issues, it can also lead to some crimes and criminals being "glorified" or mythologized.

Crimes, particularly those that attract media and public attention, have a significant impact on society—from changes in laws to influences on culture and social relationships to increased surveillance. These changes reveal how delicate the balance is between security and civil liberties, and how much depends on society's response to dramatic events.

Trauma After Crime: Psychological Impact on Victims and Families

Crimes leave lasting effects not only on the victims themselves but also on their families and loved ones. Experiencing violence or tragedy can cause profound trauma that impacts mental, physical, and social well-being. Trauma from crime, particularly when severe, is a complex phenomenon that can have long-lasting consequences and often requires specialized support. In this section, we will discuss common psychological effects of crime and coping mechanisms for those affected.

- Post-Traumatic Stress Disorder (PTSD)

PTSD is one of the most common effects of trauma following a crime, manifesting in various ways: recurrent nightmares, flashbacks (vivid, sudden memories of the traumatic event), and avoidance of places, people, or situations associated with the crime. Those with PTSD may also experience sleep disturbances, concentration issues, and sudden anxiety reactions.

For instance, survivors of assault or violent attacks often avoid locations that remind them of the event, and even specific sounds or smells associated with the trauma can trigger panic attacks.

- Depression and Hopelessness

Experiencing crime can lead to depression, marked by feelings of sadness, loss of interest in daily activities, and even suicidal thoughts. Many affected by tragedy feel an overwhelming sense of hopelessness, struggling with the emotional burden of loss or pain from the crime.

Depression can affect both survivors and the families of victims who mourn the loss of a loved one. In some cases, they may also experience secondary depression from witnessing a loved one's suffering or feeling powerless over their own emotions.

- Anxiety Disorders and Phobias

Experiencing crime can trigger various anxiety disorders that disrupt daily life. Survivors may develop new phobias, such as a fear of the dark, crowds, strangers, or even leaving the house. These fears are a defensive reaction by the body, attempting to protect itself from similar future events.

For example, someone who has survived an assault may fear being alone in public spaces. Such anxieties can limit their freedom, strain relationships, and lead to social isolation.

- Survivor's Guilt

Individuals who survive traumatic events, especially when others have lost their lives, may experience survivor's guilt. This often affects people who have lived through disasters, attacks, or have witnessed the deaths of loved ones. The guilt stems from thoughts that they "could have done more" or that "they should have been the one to die," leading to intense grief and difficulty coping with trauma.

In families of murder victims, survivor's guilt can manifest as a belief that the tragedy could have been prevented. Loved ones may question what they could have done differently, which can lead to depression and a feeling of losing control over life.

- Impact on Family and Social Relationships

Crime-related trauma can have a negative impact on family relationships. Those affected often withdraw emotionally, becoming distant and finding it hard to maintain connections, even with close family members. Victims' families may struggle to communicate and support one another, leading to deepening isolation and heightened tension within the family.

Loved ones may also experience "secondary trauma," sharing in the victim's pain. Sometimes, trauma affects entire communities, as in high-profile crimes where one family's suffering resonates with many others.

- ### The Need for Psychological Support and Trauma Therapy

In many cases, psychological support and therapy are crucial. Professionals help victims and their families manage symptoms of PTSD, depression, or anxiety, enabling them to function better in daily life. Trauma therapy, especially cognitive-behavioral therapy (CBT) and EMDR (Eye Movement Desensitization and Reprocessing), can aid in processing traumatic memories and developing healthy coping mechanisms.

For many victims and their loved ones, social support—such as support groups where they can share experiences with others who have endured similar trauma—is also essential. Support from others who understand their emotions provides acceptance and facilitates healing.

Crime-related trauma is complex, requiring long-term work and support. For victims and their families, the journey to regain psychological balance is a difficult one that often calls for professional assistance. Increasing public awareness of these effects and developing support programs are essential to helping those affected return to as normal a life as possible.

The Role of Media in Shaping the Perception of Crime

Media have a powerful impact on how we perceive the world, particularly when it comes to crime. High-profile trials, murders, or thefts reach millions of people, shaping their opinions on safety, justice, and police actions. In this section, we'll examine how media influence public perception of crime and the potential consequences of that influence.

- ### The "Shock and Sensation" Effect

Media often attract viewers through dramatic headlines and sensational coverage of crimes, creating both interest and fear. Stories about brutal murders, kidnappings, or terrorist attacks appear far more frequently in the news than minor offenses. This "shock and sensation" effect gives the impression that crime is more frequent and violent, raising public anxiety about safety.

An example is the case of a young girl's murder, which was reported as the tragedy of an "ideal victim." Such portrayals focus viewers' attention on the victim and evoke strong emotions, which shape public opinion and heighten a sense of threat.

- Creating Stereotypes and Demonizing Perpetrators

Media tend to portray certain types of offenders in a consistently negative light, often leading to stereotyping. Offenders in racially, ethnically, or economically motivated crimes may be demonized, with certain traits ascribed to them that contribute to biases against entire social groups.

In the U.S., this can be seen in cases involving African Americans or immigrants, where media focus on negative aspects of the perpetrator's background, fostering unfair stereotypes. A similar pattern can be observed in Poland, where certain minority groups may be disproportionately portrayed as criminal.

- Heightened Fear and the "Culture of Fear"

Constant media coverage of crime can contribute to a "culture of fear," where people believe crime to be more widespread than it is. Frequent reporting on incidents like robberies, murders, or attacks can make society feel more endangered, even if crime rates are declining.

In response, media inadvertently (or deliberately) influence government policies, as social concerns prompt governments to allocate more funds for law enforcement or enact harsher penalties. This can lead to political actions such as increased surveillance or the implementation of stricter criminal penalties.

- Shaping the Image of Victims and Public Empathy

Media not only influence how we view perpetrators but also how we perceive victims. Victims' stories are often presented in ways that evoke empathy and compassion, and sometimes even mythologize their lives. Media's choice of which victims to cover can also introduce bias—stories of young, attractive women are more likely to be highlighted, while cases involving older people or those on society's margins are often overlooked.

This selective portrayal can lead to "selective empathy," where only certain victims are met with societal sympathy, while others are overlooked or minimized.

- Media's Role in Spreading Conspiracy Theories

In some cases, media contribute to the spread of conspiracy theories. Notable examples include cases such as President Kennedy's assassination or Marilyn Monroe's death, often reported as "mysterious" or filled with "suspicious details." This portrayal can fuel public doubt regarding law enforcement and promote theories that further shape public opinion.

As a result, such theories can erode public trust in law enforcement and the justice system, leading to increased skepticism toward court decisions.

- The True Crime Culture and Its Social Impact

The popularity of crime documentaries, podcasts, and true crime shows has brought crime into popular culture. On one hand, this trend can educate the public about dangers and criminal behaviors, but on the other hand, it risks "honoring" criminals by granting them media attention.

True crime culture has a dual impact: it broadens awareness of criminal methods, yet can also encourage fascination with violence. In some instances, movies or shows can even inspire copycat crimes, as with murders inspired by the "Zodiac" character.

Thus, media play an immense role in shaping the perception of crime. The balance of ethical reporting and social responsibility determines whether society receives reliable information or falls under the influence of sensationalism and fear. Raising public awareness and maintaining respect for victims while reporting on crime is essential for balanced media coverage.

11. Criminal Quotes and Facts

Guess the Quote: Who Said It?

The words spoken by criminals, victims, detectives, or judges can reveal much about their motivations, personalities, and sometimes even shock with their intensity. In this section, readers are invited to guess the authors of famous criminal quotes and learn how these words have impacted the history of criminology.

Each quote is paired with multiple choice options, and the answers provide a brief context to give readers a deeper understanding of the crime and events surrounding the quote.

Quote Selections and Analysis

"This is the last thing I see before I close my eyes."

Context: Operating in California during the 1980s, he became infamous for his brutality and sadistic approach to his victims. His words convey a specific type of cruelty and fascination with evil that defined his criminal career.

Answer Choices:

A) Ted Bundy

B) Charles Manson

C) Richard Ramirez

D) Jeffrey Dahmer

- "I don't regret what I did. I only regret getting caught."

Context: One of the most notorious serial killers, confessed to the brutal murders of at least 30 young women. This quote reflects his lack of remorse and narcissistic view of his actions.

Answer Choices:

A) Richard Kuklinski

B) Ted Bundy

C) David Berkowitz

D) Albert Fish

- ### "When you kill, you feel like God."

Context: Active serial killer in the 1970s, expressed his dark perspective on crime through this quote, underscoring his psychological issues and need for control.

Answer Choices:

A) Richard Ramirez

B) Edmund Kemper

C) John Wayne Gacy

D) Charles Manson

- ### "If I Did It, Here's How It Happened."

Context: The title of .... book, which describes hypothetical details of the murder of his ex-wife and her friend, despite his official non-admission of guilt, sparked significant controversy and public debate.

Answer Choices:

A) Robert Blake

B) Scott Peterson

C) O.J. Simpson

D) Aaron Hernandez

- ### "I found killing to be more enjoyable than sex."

Context: Known for his cruelty and deviant tendencies, ... statement reflects his severe psychological disorders and sadistic approach to life. His crimes remain among the most brutal in history.

Answer Choices:

A) Richard Kuklinski

B) Jeffrey Dahmer

C) Albert Fish

D) David Berkowitz

Identify the Crime from the Description

In this section, readers will test their knowledge of history's most infamous crimes by matching descriptions of key cases with the criminal or specific event involved. Each description will include critical details about the criminal's modus operandi, victims, or location, enabling readers to put their criminological insight into practice.

Sample Crime Descriptions:

Description: "On a warm summer evening in California, a brutal crime took place against a young actress who was home with friends. The intruders left bloody traces and a message scrawled in blood on the wall. Among the perpetrators was the leader of a cult, who inspired his followers to commit these crimes."

Answer: ...

Description: "In the late 1960s and early 70s, a mysterious killer operated in San Francisco, sending encrypted messages to newspapers, taunting the police and the public. This criminal left few clues, and their identity remains unknown to this day. The killer is known to have murdered at least five people, and a unique symbol resembling a crosshair became their signature."

Answer: ...

Description: "The body of a young girl was found in a cramped, neglected room. Investigations revealed she had been imprisoned and abused by her captor for many years. The case surfaced when the victim was accidentally discovered by bystanders, sparking massive media coverage and discussions on protective measures against similar crimes."

Answer: ...

Description: "A young man traveled across the United States, murdering women in several states. The killer gained his victims' trust by appearing helpful. He was handsome and well-mannered, leading the victims to believe he was safe. Ultimately, he confessed to the murder of over 30 women."

Answer: ...

Description: "In a small town on the city outskirts, several young men's bodies were found. The investigation revealed that the killer frequently met his victims in bars and invited them back to his home, where he later murdered them. The perpetrator was a quiet, unassuming man who lived alone."

Answer: ...

Description: "A young woman was returning home one evening in New York when she was attacked. Despite there being many witnesses, no one responded to her cries for help. This incident became a symbol of social apathy and inspired research into crowd psychology."

Answer: ...

Interactive Task: Match the Crime to the Criminal or Event

Description: "A wealthy woman was found dead in her Los Angeles home, and the crime appeared meticulously planned. The investigation revealed that the perpetrator repeatedly attempted to cover their tracks at the crime scene, turning the case into a media spectacle."

A) Murder of Nicole Brown Simpson

B) Hinterkaifeck Farm Murders

C) Crime on Cielo Drive

D) The Black Dahlia Case (Elizabeth Short)

Answer: ...

Sample Knowledge Test Questions:

- Which famous crime victim led to the creation of "Megan's Law" in the USA?

    A) Megan Kanka

    B) Elizabeth Smart

    C) Polly Klaas

    D) Jaycee Dugard

    Answer: ...

Description: Seven-year-old .... was murdered by a neighbor who was a registered sex offender. Her death led to the introduction of "Megan's Law," requiring registration and public disclosure of sex offenders in the community.

- What nickname was used for serial killer David Berkowitz?

    A) Son of Sam

    B) Zodiac

    C) Green River Killer

    D) Night Stalker

    Answer: ...

Description: David Berkowitz, known as the .... terrorized New York in the 1970s by killing random individuals. His nickname came from the letters he wrote to the police, signed as................

Who was the murder victim who became a symbol of the fight against domestic violence and an inspiration for campaigns to protect women?

    A) Kitty Genovese

    B) Nicole Brown Simpson

    C) Sharon Tate

    D) Elisabeth Fritzl

    Answer: ...

Description: The death of ...., brutally murdered ex-wife of O.J. Simpson, brought attention to the issue of domestic violence. Her story sparked discussions about victim rights and the need for protection from abusive partners.

- Which serial killer earned the nickname "The Milwaukee Cannibal"?

    A) Jeffrey Dahmer

    B) Ted Bundy

    C) Ed Gein

    D) Albert Fish

    Answer: ...

Description: .... murdered and consumed parts of his victims' bodies. His case horrified the public both due to the number of his victims and the extreme brutality of his actions.

- Who was the leader of the cult responsible for the brutal murders at actress Sharon Tate's home?

    A) Charles Manson

    B) Jim Jones

    C) David Koresh

    D) Richard Ramirez

    Answer: ...

Description: .... manipulated his followers, inspiring them to commit brutal murders meant to symbolize his belief in an impending apocalyptic war. The case shocked the world and defined the image of cult culture in the 1960s and 70s.

- Which infamous case from New York in the 1960s became a symbol of the "bystander effect," reflecting social apathy in moments of crisis?

    A) Kitty Genovese Case

    B) Patty Hearst Case

C) Jaycee Dugard Case

D) Sharon Tate Case

Answer: ...

Description: The murder of .... shocked society not only because of its brutality but also due to the lack of intervention from bystanders who heard her cries for help. This case led to research on the "bystander effect" and reflections on social responsibility.

Which victim was held captive in a basement for 24 years by her father?

A) Jaycee Dugard

B) Amanda Berry

C) Elisabeth Fritzl

D) Polly Klaas

Answer: ...

Description: ....I was held captive by her father in a basement in Austria for 24 years, during which she bore several children. Her case shocked the world and prompted debates about domestic abuse and victim rights.

Shocking Facts and Statistics about Serial Killers

In this section, readers will uncover lesser-known facts and statistics about serial killers from around the world. We'll delve into unusual methods, surprising details about their lives, and statistics that reveal the scale of their crimes. Each fact sheds new light on the complex and diverse phenomenon of serial murder.

- The Country with the Most Serial Killers...

Contrary to popular belief that serial killers are primarily an American phenomenon, they are found worldwide. Serial murder cases have been recorded on every inhabited continent. Interestingly, one country with one of the highest rates of serial killers per million people is South Africa, where cases are often linked to challenging social and economic conditions, influencing individual psychological and social issues.

- The Longest-Operating Serial Killer: Javed Iqbal (Pakistan)

Javed Iqbal, one of the most terrifying serial killers, operated in Pakistan during the 1990s. He confessed to murdering 100 boys in Lahore and described his crimes in a detailed letter to the police. His activity is horrifying not only for the number of victims but also for the extended period over which he managed to evade capture. Though sentenced, Iqbal committed suicide in prison before his death sentence could be carried out.

- "Tukdam" - The Monks' Killer, Russia

Alexander Pichushkin, called "Tukdam" by Russians (a term for monks meditating on death), was one of Russia's most brutal serial killers. He killed at least 49 people with the goal of "completing the chessboard" with victims. His crimes spanned over a decade, and he marked each victim on a chessboard, intending to place 64 "pawns" representing his victims.

- The World's Youngest Serial Killer: Amarjeet Sada (India)

Amarjeet Sada from India is considered the world's youngest serial killer, committing his first murder at the age of just eight. Over a year, he killed three children, including his own sister, cousin, and a neighbor's child.

Sada's case was highly controversial, as his age made him legally a minor, exempting him from being sentenced as an adult.

- The "Vampire of Bucharest": Ion Rîmaru (Romania)

Ion Rîmaru, known as the "Vampire of Bucharest," terrorized Romania in the 1970s. His modus operandi involved attacking solitary women during storms and early mornings in Bucharest. Rîmaru also reportedly had a fascination with blood, earning him his infamous nickname. His brutal acts terrified the residents of Romania's capital, and his crimes remain a source of fear even today.

- The Serial Killer Who Inspired the Word "Strangler": Thug Behram (India)

Thug Behram, one of the most notorious serial killers in Indian history, operated at the turn of the 18th century. He was part of the "Thug" sect (which inspired the word "strangler"), responsible for approximately 900 murders through strangulation and burial. The Thugs, with whom Behram worked, believed their actions brought spiritual benefits, adding a quasi-religious dimension to their crimes.

- Astonishing Time without Capture: Pedro Alonso López (Colombia, Ecuador, Peru)

Pedro Alonso López, known as the "Monster of the Andes," was a prominent serial killer in South America, operating across Colombia, Ecuador, and Peru. López confessed to killing over 300 young girls, though many of his victims were never found. The most shocking statistic is that despite his numerous crimes and arrest in 1980, López was released after only 18 years due to sentencing limits in Ecuador, and his whereabouts remain unknown.

- Austria's Unassuming Murderess: Elfriede Blauensteiner, the "Black Widow"

Elfriede Blauensteiner became known as Austria's "Black Widow," using her relationships with wealthy men, whom she later killed for their money. In the 1990s, Blauensteiner poisoned at least three partners, and shockingly, she continued to seek new victims, convinced her plan would remain undetected.

- **The "Soap-Maker of Correggio" with the Most Documented Female Victims: Leonarda Cianciulli (Italy)**

Leonarda Cianciulli, known as the "Soap-Maker of Correggio," was an Italian serial killer who murdered at least three women in the 1940s. Her modus operandi included dissolving her victims' bodies and turning them into soap and cakes, which she then offered to neighbors. Cianciulli's story horrified Italy, becoming one of Europe's most macabre cases of serial murder.

- **The Highest Number of Victims Attributed to a Family of Killers: The Bender Family (USA)**

In the mid-19th century, the Bender family terrorized travelers in Kansas, operating an inn where they killed guests who stayed overnight. It's estimated that the Benders killed around 12 people, though this number may be much higher, as bodies were found long after their disappearances. The family was never apprehended, and their story inspired many horror tales.

Random Facts about Serial Killers

This section is a collection of random facts, anecdotes, and curiosities related to serial killers that may shock, intrigue, or even fascinate. Each subsection contains information on lesser-known criminals from various parts of the world.

- **Which Killer Did This?**

In this part, match unusual acts or signature behaviors with the specific killer. Each description provides a fact about a criminal, and readers' task is to guess which murderer it corresponds to.

Examples:

Which murderer used poison and was one of the longest-operating serial killers in France?

A) Dr. Marcel Petiot

B) Jeanne Weber

C) Henri Désiré Landru

D) Gilles de Rais

Answer: …

Description: Known as the .... operated in the early 20th century, poisoning at least 10 women he met through marriage ads. He hid his crimes for years until he was finally convicted and executed by guillotine.

- Which serial killer was obsessed with fashion and designed outfits for a doll made from the remains of his victims?

   A) Anatoly Moskvin

   B) La Bestia

   C) Tsutomu Miyazaki

   D) Adolfo Constanzo

   Answer: …

Description: Known as the "Mummy" in Russia, ... had a strange fixation with dolls and mummification. He kept mummified bodies of young girls in his apartment, dressing them in specially designed outfits and treating them as his "dolls."

- Which criminal used a refrigerator to store body parts of his victims in his apartment in Germany?

   A) Joachim Kroll

   B) Fritz Haarmann

   C) Carl Großmann

   D) Armin Meiwes

   Answer: …

Description: Known as the "Duisburg Cannibal," .... killed more than a dozen people in the 1950s and 60s. He kept body parts in his refrigerator, later using them to prepare meals.

True or False – Shocking Facts About Criminals

In this section, you'll decide whether each statement is true or false. Each fact provides an unusual detail or story about serial killers, allowing a closer look at surprising aspects of their lives and crimes.

Examples:

Question: "The serial killer Albert DeSalvo, known as the 'Boston Strangler,' attempted to sell the rights to his story for a film even before his arrest."

Answer: True/False

Question: "Luis Garavito, known as 'La Bestia,' murdered over 200 children in Colombia and, after his arrest, joined campaigns to protect children's rights."

Answer: True/False

Question: "Serial killer Anatoly Onoprienko, called the 'Beast of Ukraine,' was a computer technician before starting his criminal career."

Answer: True/False

Question: "Pedro Rodrigues Filho, a Brazilian serial killer known as the 'Pied Piper of Brazil,' only murdered other criminals."

Answer: True/False

Question: "The infamous killer Charles Manson never personally committed any of the murders for which he was convicted; instead, he ordered his followers to carry them out."

Answer: True/False

Curiosities and Lesser-Known Facts About Infamous Criminals

Here, you'll find some lesser-known facts and surprising details about notorious serial killers. These insights may shock or intrigue you, offering a deeper look into the complex minds of infamous criminals.

- Kazuo Shinozawa – "The Elevator Killer" (Japan)

Kazuo Shinozawa, known as "The Elevator Killer," terrorized Japanese high-rises in the 1980s by attacking unsuspecting victims in elevator shafts. He targeted random people in this confined space, where he felt total control. His crimes spread fear across Japan, making him one of the country's first infamous serial killers.

- Issei Sagawa – The Killer Who Became a Celebrity (Japan)

Issei Sagawa committed murder and cannibalism while studying in Paris, yet when deported to Japan, he avoided prison time entirely. Astonishingly, Sagawa became a well-known media figure in Japan, publishing books, appearing on talk shows, and even reviewing food for magazines.

- Fritz Honka – "The Hamburg Woman Killer" (Germany)

Known as "The Hamburg Woman Killer," Fritz Honka murdered several women in the 1970s, hiding their remains in his small apartment. His secret life unraveled when a fire broke out, and firefighters found bodies. The shocking discovery ended Honka's violent spree and left Germany in disbelief.

- Peter Sutcliffe – "The Yorkshire Ripper" (England)

Peter Sutcliffe terrorized northern England in the 1970s, attacking women and evading capture for years. Known as "The Yorkshire Ripper," Sutcliffe's crimes forced Britain to reform how police approached serial cases, highlighting flaws that had let him slip through law enforcement's grasp for so long.

- Martha Rendell – "The Wicked Stepmother" (Australia)

Martha Rendell, one of Australia's rare female serial killers, murdered her partner's three children in the 1930s by giving them irritants disguised as medicine, inducing symptoms of a fatal illness. Rendell's crimes were publicized widely, and she became the first woman to be executed in Australia.

- Andrei Chikatilo – "The Butcher of Rostov" (Russia)

Andrei Chikatilo was one of the most prolific serial killers in Soviet history, responsible for at least 52 brutal murders from the late 1970s to the early 1990s. Known as "The Butcher of Rostov," Chikatilo evaded authorities for years due to investigative missteps and limited forensic technology. His chilling crimes were among the first to raise public awareness of serial murder in the USSR.

- Amelia Dyer – "The Baby Butcher" (England)

In Victorian England, Amelia Dyer ran a so-called "baby farming" business, where she accepted infants from struggling mothers with the promise of a better life for the children. Instead, Dyer was responsible for the deaths of hundreds of infants in her care over a span of decades. Her eventual arrest and conviction in 1896 horrified the nation and spurred new child protection laws in England.

- Carl Panzram – "The Outlaw Killer" (United States)

Carl Panzram, a drifter and violent criminal in early 20th-century America, confessed to a string of murders and assaults across multiple countries. His journal, where he vividly described his hatred for humanity and his crimes, shocked readers. Panzram's story highlighted gaps in the penal system's handling of violent offenders and remains one of the most disturbing accounts of a serial killer's psyche.

- Jane Toppan – "Jolly Jane" (United States)

Jane Toppan, a nurse in the late 19th century, confessed to killing at least 31 patients in Massachusetts. Known as "Jolly Jane" for her cheerful demeanor, she used her position to administer fatal doses of morphine and atropine to unsuspecting patients, often staying by their side to watch their reactions. Toppan's case shocked the medical community and led to heightened awareness about the potential dangers of unchecked authority in caregiving roles.

10. Quiz: "Which Murderer?"

In this activity, you'll receive a list of facts detailing the unusual behaviors or actions of serial killers. Your challenge is to match each fact to the correct murderer from a set of options. To make it challenging, some facts may be lesser-known or describe unique details that require in-depth knowledge or insights detectives focused on.

Example:

Fact: "Which serial killer used his profession as a bakery owner to hide victims' bodies in the bakery building and then sent food packages to their families?"

Options:

A) Carl Großmann (Germany)

B) Fritz Honka (Germany)

C) Andrei Chikatilo (Russia)

D) Joachim Kroll (Germany)

Answer: …

Explanation: ...., a bakery owner in Berlin, hid bodies in his bakery, making his case one of Berlin's darkest criminal episodes.

Fact: "Which murderer considered himself a 'savior' of women, believing his killings were a mission to 'free' women from suffering?"

Options:

A) Michel Fourniret (France)

B) Jack Unterweger (Austria)

C) Robert Hansen (Alaska, USA)

D) Charles Sobhraj (India)

Answer: …

Explanation: .... serial killer, claimed he was "freeing" women through his murders. His case was extremely controversial, as he was released after his first sentence, only to resume his crimes.

True or False

This task challenges you to decide whether each fact is true or false, giving you a chance to explore unusual or shocking information about serial killers. Each fact provides a unique detail, adding intrigue but possibly leading you astray. After each response, you'll receive an explanation confirming (or debunking) the fact.

Examples:

Question: "Serial killer Pedro Alonso López, 'The Monster of the Andes,' after his release worked as a security advisor on Colombian television."

True or False: ...

Question: "John Christie, a British serial killer, kept his victims' bodies behind his apartment wall for several years without raising his neighbors' suspicions."

True or False: ...

Guess Who? "Did You Know?"

In this quiz, you're invited to guess the country or cultural background associated with each described case. This task highlights the diversity of serial killer cases worldwide, revealing less familiar aspects of crime in different regions. Each fact is presented without a specific perpetrator, so you'll rely on options to identify the correct context.

Examples:

Curiosity: "This killer sent letters to victims' families after his crimes, describing in detail what he had done to increase their suffering. His actions sparked panic in the local community."

Options:

A) Japan

B) Russia

C) India

D) United Kingdom

Answer: ...

Curiosity: "This female killer used poison to eliminate her partners and was known for a unique approach to her victims—she hosted dinners and offered expensive gifts before she killed."

Options:

A) France

B) Brazil

C) Poland

D) Italy

Answer: ...

Curiosity: "He believed his crimes were directed by an evil spirit he controlled, committing murders as a way to 'purify.'"

Options:

A) Haiti

B) Philippines

C) Nigeria

D) Egypt

Answer: ...

Curiosity: "This killer posed as a traveling salesman, using his charm to earn the trust of his victims before luring them to secluded locations. He operated across multiple states, making it difficult for authorities to track him."

Options:

A) Germany

B) United States

C) Canada

D) France

Answer: ...

Curiosity: "This murderer claimed he was driven by a mystical vision to 'cleanse' his city of sin. Known for a distinctive calling card left at crime scenes, he evoked both fascination and fear among locals."

Options:

A) Italy

B) Russia

C) Argentina

D) South Africa

Answer: …

Curiosity: "This murderer targeted members of his own family, eliminating relatives one by one over the course of several years to inherit the family wealth. His meticulous methods and calm demeanor kept suspicions at bay for years."

Options:

A) United States

B) France

C) Italy

D) Japan

Answer: …

Curiosity: "Known as the 'Killer Clown,' this murderer was popular in his community, often performing at children's parties in his clown costume. No one suspected that his cheerful persona hid a dark side."

Options:

A) Canada

B) United States

C) Australia

D) United Kingdom

Answer: …

11. The Ultimate Test: Criminal Challenge

This is the final test of your detective skills! In this challenge, you'll face a series of criminal cases and mysteries designed to test your knowledge, reasoning, and ability to connect clues. Will you be able to piece together the evidence, see through alibis, and uncover the truth? Prepare to dive into complex cases that will push your investigative skills to the limit.

Solve the Crime Mystery: Create Your Own Scenario Based on Clues

Imagine you're the lead investigator assigned to a mysterious murder case that took place in a quiet suburban neighborhood. You have a list of clues and evidence at your disposal. Your task is to piece together all the elements, analyze the evidence, and build a scenario that explains what really happened.

The Case

In a home within a peaceful suburb, the body of Michael Wallis, a 34-year-old businessman, has been found. Known as a calm, unassuming individual, Michael's life reveals hidden complexities as you dive deeper into the case. At the crime scene, you find clues that bring some clarity but also raise more questions.

Are you up for the challenge?

Clues

Blood Trails:

Blood traces in the hallway lead in two directions: toward the kitchen and upstairs to the bedroom. Analysis shows not all blood belongs to Michael. Could this mean the perpetrator was injured, or perhaps someone else was present?

The Kitchen Phone:

Michael's phone was found in the kitchen. His last call was made one hour before his death — a short call to his wife, who was away visiting friends. In the background, faint footsteps and the sound of a struggle can be heard. What might have been happening during this call?

Note in the Bedroom:

On the bedside table, there's a note with the address of Robert Kane, a family friend. It has a handwritten addendum: "we need to talk." Could Robert be involved? What could the note mean?

Neighbors' Testimonies:

Neighbors claim they heard voices arguing from Michael's house around 11 p.m. They also noticed a dark-tinted car parked nearby, which is unusual for such a quiet area. Could the sounds and movements heard during the phone call relate to these reports?

A Lost Glove:

A single glove lies near the back exit of the house. It doesn't belong to Michael, and it's too worn out to retrieve any fingerprints. Nearby, you also find a cigarette butt of an unusual brand. Coincidence, or a planted diversion?

Ledger in the Office:

In Michael's office, you discover a ledger filled with entries documenting payouts to Robert Kane over the last two months, suggesting possible financial trouble. What could this reveal about Michael and Robert's relationship?

Your Task

Using the clues above, try to answer the following questions and create your own crime scenario:

Who is your primary suspect and why?

Analyze the relationships between Michael, his wife, and his friend Robert. Do the clues suggest that the perpetrator acted out of revenge, jealousy, or financial motive?

What do the neighbors' statements imply?

Since they reported hearing footsteps and voices, could someone have been inside the house before the police arrived? Was the suspicious car related to the incident?

Are the note and ledger essential to the case?

If Robert Kane is involved, what does it say about his relationship with Michael? Could Michael's financial problems have led to a conflict?

What do the phone call and sounds of struggle suggest?

Imagine what might have happened during Michael's last call to his wife. Could the footsteps heard on the recording indicate the presence of an unwelcome guest?

What could the glove and cigarette butt mean?

Are they traces left behind by the perpetrator, or could they be distractions planted to mislead investigators?

Build the Most Likely Scenario

Based on everything you know, create a possible sequence of events for the night of the murder. Was there a dispute with his friend, or could it have been revenge by a third party?

Your Conclusion

Once you've developed a scenario, consider a few possible conclusions:

Scenario A: The murder was the result of a financial dispute between Michael and Robert, leading to a heated confrontation and a crime of passion.

Scenario B: The crime was orchestrated by an outsider with a vendetta against Michael, using his financial troubles to cover their tracks.

Scenario C: The murder stemmed from a complex personal relationship involving Michael and someone close to him, driven by jealousy or revenge.

Solving this mystery allows you to create your own crime-solving scenario, connecting pieces of evidence to potential motives. Your thoughts and analysis could lead to different conclusions, each bringing you closer to understanding how detectives unravel real-life cases!

Choose Your Detective Path: How Will You Solve the Mystery?

This time, you're the one in charge of how the investigation unfolds! As the lead detective, you have access to evidence collected at the crime scene and witness statements. Your mission is to decide which investigative path to take to piece together the mystery and identify the killer. Each step could either bring you closer to the truth—or lead you astray.

In this interactive case, you'll face critical choices that will determine the direction of your investigation. Prepare for some unexpected twists!

Mystery Scenario: "Murder at the Train Station"

Case Background:

On a chilly winter morning, a man's body is discovered at a quiet suburban train station. The victim, 34-year-old Michael Wallis, was a local businessman known for his calm demeanor. Initial evidence hints at a struggle, but it's up to you to connect the dots.

The scene reveals clues leading in multiple directions, and witness testimonies are conflicting. Your careful decisions will determine whether you uncover the truth.

Investigative Paths

Step 1: Which Clue Do You Analyze First?

Option A: Bootprints in the frozen ground leading toward the train tracks.

Option B: The victim's phone with a recent call from an unknown number made only minutes before his death.

Option C: A broken branch near the crime scene, suggesting someone was hiding.

Each choice leads to different insights:

If you choose A (bootprints): You notice the footprints are too large to belong to the victim. This suggests the suspect fled toward the tracks, possibly signaling an attempted getaway on foot or that an accomplice was waiting nearby.

If you choose B (phone): You trace the call to a close associate of the victim who had recently worked with Michael. This leads you to question what was so urgent that he called minutes before the murder.

If you choose C (broken branch): You infer someone may have been lying in wait for Michael. This suggests the crime might have been planned in advance.

Step 2: Who Do You Interview First?

Option A: A passenger waiting for the morning train who claims to have seen a masked figure leaving the scene in a hurry.

Option B: A close friend of the victim who denies involvement but had frequent recent conversations with Michael.

Option C: The station attendant who claims he overheard what sounded like an argument moments before Michael's death.

Each choice offers more perspective:

If you choose A (passenger): The witness describes the masked figure wearing a dark coat and carrying a heavy object—perhaps a weapon? He also claims the person entered a car parked nearby.

If you choose B (close friend): The friend appears nervous, evading questions about his recent conversations with Michael but mentions that Michael had been anxious about someone at work.

If you choose C (station attendant): The attendant describes hearing two voices—one he thought was Michael, the other low and angry, hinting at a heated argument.

Step 3: Establishing Motive

Option A: Focus on financial motives. Checking Michael's bank account, you find odd withdrawals, possibly indicating debts or blackmail.

Option B: Explore personal conflicts. Interviews with Michael's coworkers reveal tensions between him and another employee.

Option C: Analyze his recent messages to learn more about his contacts with friends and family.

Choose carefully, as each path opens new possibilities:

If you choose A (financial motive): You discover Michael had substantial debts owed to a person linked to local criminal activity, suggesting possible motives related to money.

If you choose B (personal conflict): You learn Michael and a coworker had a recent confrontation that turned physical. Could emotions have escalated further?

If you choose C (recent messages): You find threatening messages that Michael received over the past few weeks but chose not to report, hinting at hidden fears.

Your Investigation: Make the Final Decision

Using the evidence you've gathered, develop a working theory on what happened at the train station.

Motive: Was this a random attack, calculated revenge, or a conflict rooted in money issues?

Suspect: Did the person you suspect have a strong enough motive? Which clues point directly to this individual?

Events: Envision how the crime played out—how might the suspect have planned and executed the attack based on the clues?

Possible Endings:

Ending A: You conclude that the murder stemmed from financial conflicts. Michael was killed by someone to whom he owed a significant debt, with the scene staged to obscure the real motive.

Ending B: You deduce that jealousy led a coworker to act out of fear that Michael might tarnish his reputation, resulting in a violent altercation.

Ending C: You discover it was an impulsive attack, sparked by a personal argument, and all clues point to a close associate of the victim.

Your investigation reveals how detectives must make strategic choices and analyze evidence step by step. By choosing different paths, you explore various angles and scenarios, ultimately working your way toward uncovering what really happened at the train station.

The Ultimate Crime and Forensics Knowledge Test

This final section challenges you to see how much you truly know about famous crimes, forensics, and landmark investigations that changed history. This quiz is designed to help you recap key information from previous chapters and test your knowledge on new topics within forensics.

Each question is an opportunity to deepen your understanding of the fascinating world of detectives and investigations—and who knows, it may even inspire you to explore the topic further!

Questions:

- Which of the following techniques is most effective for detecting invisible traces of blood?

    A) Using luminol

    B) Screening with ultraviolet light

    C) Applying fingerprint powders

    D) DNA analysis

    Answer: …

- Which type of evidence best identifies a specific perpetrator?

    A) Shoe prints

    B) Tire tracks

    C) Fingerprints

    D) Witness statements

    Answer: …

- Which serial killer is commonly regarded as the 'father of criminal profiling'?

A) Ted Bundy

B) Jack Unterweger

C) David Berkowitz

D) John Douglas

Answer: ...

- Who was the first person in legal history to be convicted using DNA analysis?

    A) Colin Pitchfork

    B) Jeffrey MacDonald

    C) Albert DeSalvo

    D) Richard Ramirez

    Answer: ...

- What is the name of the crime scene analysis method focused on studying the angles and directions of blood spatter?

    A) Dactyloscopy

    B) Ballistics

    C) Crime scene reconstruction

    D) Blood spatter analysis

    Answer: ...

Which type of evidence is crucial in cybercrime cases?

A) IP address

B) Fingerprint

C) Footprint

D) Blood analysis

Answer: ...

Interactive Test Formats:

Multiple Choice – Each question provides four options, and each answer includes a detailed explanation to help you understand the context.

True/False – Quick statements to assess as true or false, e.g., "Criminal profiling is used solely for tracking serial killers." (Answer: False – profiling is also used in cases like terrorism or assault).

Scenario Questions – Based on described scenarios, choose the best method to solve the problem, e.g., "You have a small piece of fiber found at the crime scene. What would be most useful in its analysis?" (Answer: Chemical or microscopic analysis).

Timed Challenges – To raise the stakes, some questions can be answered under time pressure, adding a layer of challenge to test how well you recall key facts under pressure.

This test is an excellent opportunity to sum up everything you've learned about forensics and famous crimes, while also testing your detective skills. If you succeed in this ultimate test, you'll know you have the knowledge and intuition that would be right at home in real investigations!

12. Solutions

Crime Puzzles and Quizzes

1. Answer: b) H.H. Holmes – In the 1890s, Holmes built a hotel, famously called the "Murder Castle," where he committed horrifying crimes

2. Answer: b) Sharon Tate's murder – Roman Polanski's pregnant wife was brutally killed along with her friends by members of Charles Manson's cult.

3. Answer: b) Zodiac – The Zodiac Killer terrorized California in the 1960s and 70s, sending encrypted messages to newspapers and mocking the police.

4. Answer: b) DNA analysis – This technology allowed investigators to solve previously unsolved cases by identifying suspects through genetic material.

5. Answer: b) 1932 – The kidnapping and murder of the famous aviator's son shocked America and drew worldwide media attention.

6. Answer: b) John Wayne Gacy – Gacy killed 33 young men, burying their bodies in the crawlspace of his house.

7. Answer: a) Night Stalker – Richard Ramirez terrorized California in the mid-1980s with a spree of brutal assaults, rapes, and murders.

Crime-Themed Puzzles and Brain Teasers

Criminal Wordsearch

Crime Scene

```
G A Z G H K F K V S Z F T K D S K U L L
E Y U Q Q Q T Q P I E V I D E N C E B A
Q O G H O W N R N R J N A V H M L F S T
P Z Y J W F X J A X K X E Y N S R U C F
R U L W H F W W V C N A B X G T R W R J
O E K X M W U E R C E Q X H W Q O M U L
S A Z W K D X U I J Q L D G W P Q O E V
Y M P N S T G A W L O H R T C S L O D I
H M R O L W K K K W T Q F Z H B C H S B
S Y J K A A V Z Q D Q S H O N Y H K E V
U Q R S D P C T N D Q S E E Q D V W A X
Y H O I P U N D M R G E Q N G P I Y A Q
F O G R Q W W J C U B N J U U R F C W U
W W C N V R E C O N S T R U C T I O N D
H B F D L K Q H B G F I G T C L U E S O
Z Y O Q Q M O F B X K W P R I N T S S F
L O A V C G Y T B L O O D S T A I N R W
Z N M S L B J Y R A P K L N V H J S F D
B T Z G Q W W D O C J U L C M V F Y K Y
M Y B T F A R B C E L P O L I C E F W X
```

Criminal Profiling

```
O Y E E E A G W A V M J W K L X Z E W J
A N G T M E M Y I Y P S Y C H O L O G Y
G T X C C M W O R P K W Q R K A S J H E
G R K A P O Z E T Q U I Q I Q R S L U R
R A U R R T O E Z I P T I C B P L T Y V
E U C S E I M Q R O V D O O R J X V D R
S M O M T O Z J K Y T E O T O G F Z C F
S A G B C N T A T O C Y U W I P S G A Z
I G H K A S F K V S Z Y F T V K H D E Y
O U Q Q R Q Q P I B A S Q O A G O H O W
N N N R A J N A V H M U L F H S C T P Z
Y J W F H X J X K X E O Y N E S K R U C
F R U L C W H F W W V L N A B B X G R W
R J O E K X M W U E R A C Q X H W Q M U
B L S A Z W K D X U I E J Q L D G W P Q
E V Y M P N S T G A W U L O H R T C S L
O I H M R O L W K K K W T Q F Z H B C H
S B S Y J K A A V Z Q D Q H O N Y H K E
V U Q R S D P C T N D Q E E Q D V W A X
Y H O I P U N D M R G R E V E N G E Q N
```

116

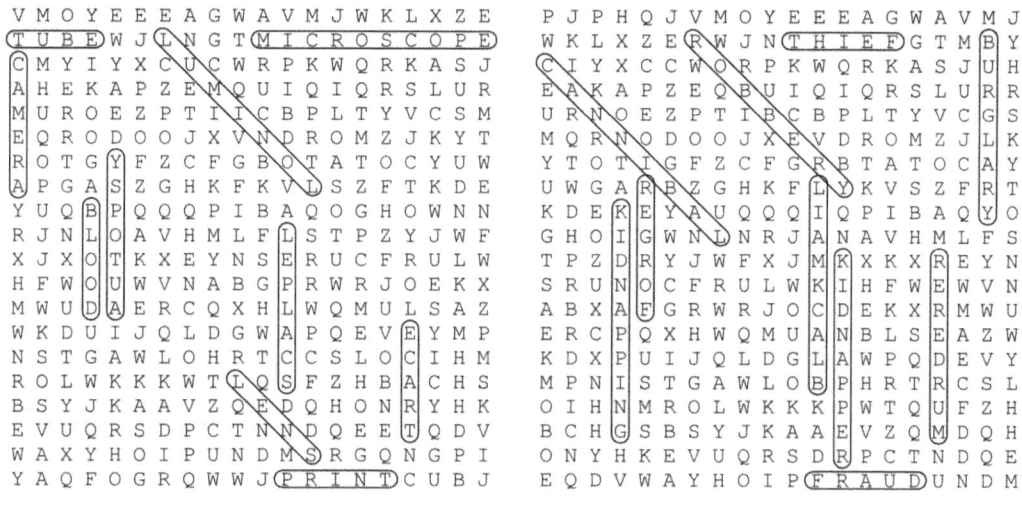

11. Criminal Quotes and Facts

Answer: C) Richard Ramirez

Description: Known for his ruthlessness, Ramirez often spoke of his fascination with evil, confirmed by this quote he shared with investigators before his trial

Answer: B) Ted Bundy

Description: Known for his manipulative and narcissistic tendencies, Bundy's lack of empathy was striking to both investigators and psychologists.

Answer: B) Edmund Kemper

Description: Kemper stood out among serial killers for his brutality and chilling self-awareness. His philosophy was dominated by a need for domination, reflected in this statement.

Answer: C) O.J. Simpson

Description: Despite his acquittal in the murder case, Simpson's book was perceived by many as an implicit confession. It remains controversial and shapes public perception of him to this day.

Answer: C) Albert Fish

Description: Fish was infamous for his sadistic treatment of victims and confessed to horrific acts of violence, which shocked society for years.

Identify the Crime from the Description

1. Comment: The Manson Family committed these murders under the influence of their leader, Charles Manson, who believed he could incite an apocalyptic racial war. The murder of Sharon Tate shocked the public and remains one of the most infamous crimes of the 20th century.

2. Comment: The Zodiac Killer is one of the most enigmatic serial murderers, with his cryptic messages and the lack of concrete evidence making this case unsolved to this day. He remains an iconic figure in pop culture.

3. Comment: Elisabeth Fritzl was held captive by her father, Josef Fritzl, in a basement for 24 years in Austria. Her case prompted discussions on children's rights, family safety, and the need for laws protecting victims of domestic violence.

4. Comment: Ted Bundy is one of history's most recognized serial killers. His intelligence, looks, and manipulative skills allowed him to gain his victims' trust, which made him even more terrifying.

5. Comment: Jeffrey Dahmer, known as the "Milwaukee Cannibal," committed gruesome murders, luring his victims into his home where he killed them. His case shocked the public due to the brutality and cannibalistic practices involved.

6. Comment: The murder of Kitty Genovese was one of the first cases widely covered by the media in the context of crowd psychology and the "bystander effect." It led to the development of the term and reflections on social responsibility.

Knowledge Test Questions:

1. Description: Seven-year-old Megan Kanka was murdered by a neighbor who was a registered sex offender. Her death led to the introduction of "Megan's Law," requiring registration and public disclosure of sex offenders in the community.

2. Description: David Berkowitz, known as the "Son of Sam," terrorized New York in the 1970s by killing random individuals. His nickname came from the letters he wrote to the police, signed as "Son of Sam."

3. Description: The death of Nicole Brown Simpson, brutally murdered ex-wife of O.J. Simpson, brought attention to the issue of domestic violence. Her story sparked discussions about victim rights and the need for protection from abusive partners.

4. Description: Dahmer murdered and consumed parts of his victims' bodies. His case horrified the public both due to the number of his victims and the extreme brutality of his actions.

5. Description: Charles Manson manipulated his followers, inspiring them to commit brutal murders meant to symbolize his belief in an impending apocalyptic war. The case shocked the world and defined the image of cult culture in the 1960s and 70s.

6. Description: The murder of Kitty Genovese shocked society not only because of its brutality but also due to the lack of intervention from bystanders who heard her cries for help. This case led to research on the "bystander effect" and reflections on social responsibility.

7. Description: Elisabeth Fritzl was held captive by her father in a basement in Austria for 24 years, during which she bore several children. Her case shocked the world and prompted debates about domestic abuse and victim rights.

Random Facts about Serial Killers

1. Description: Known as the "French Bluebeard," Landru operated in the early 20th century, poisoning at least 10 women he met through marriage ads. He hid his crimes for years until he was finally convicted and executed by guillotine.

2. Description: Known as the "Mummy" in Russia, Moskvin had a strange fixation with dolls and mummification. He kept mummified bodies of young girls in his apartment, dressing them in specially designed outfits and treating them as his "dolls."

3. Description: Known as the "Duisburg Cannibal," Kroll killed more than a dozen people in the 1950s and 60s. He kept body parts in his refrigerator, later using them to prepare meals.

True or False – Shocking Facts About Criminals

1. Description: DeSalvo, suspected of a series of murders in Boston in the 1960s, reportedly reached out to the media to profit from his notoriety—though evidence suggests he may not have committed all the murders attributed to the "Strangler."

2. Description: Although Garavito confessed to the brutal murders of hundreds of children, his sentences in Colombia were later reduced. However, he never participated in children's rights campaigns, and his crimes continue to provoke strong emotions nationwide.

3. Description: Onoprienko had no technical education or job before his crimes. His killing spree stemmed from a deep hatred for society and a desire to exert power over others.

11. Quiz: "Which Murderer?"

1. Explanation: Großmann, a bakery owner in Berlin, hid bodies in his bakery, making his case one of Berlin's darkest criminal episodes.

2. Explanation: Unterweger, an Austrian serial killer, claimed he was "freeing" women through his murders. His case was extremely controversial, as he was released after his first sentence, only to resume his crimes.

3. Explanation: Although López did regain freedom after just 18 years, he never worked in television security. His current whereabouts remain unknown, causing unease in South America.

4. Explanation: Sagawa, a notorious murderer from Japan, became infamous for his macabre messages to the victims' families, sparking widespread fear.

5. Explanation: Leonarda Cianciulli, the "Soap-Maker of Correggio," shocked Italy with her method of endearing herself to her victims. Her story remains one of Italy's most gruesome crime cases.

6. Explanation: In Haitian culture, linked to voodoo beliefs, several criminals have used religion as a justification for their actions, seeing themselves as 'vessels' for evil spirits.

7. Explanation: This Russian killer became infamous not only for his crimes but also for the unique symbol he left behind, which he believed signified a spiritual 'mission.' His story continues to haunt the memories of residents in his city.

8. Explanation: Known for his calculated approach, this American killer carefully planned each murder, ensuring it looked natural or accidental, allowing him to remain above suspicion as he methodically collected his family's inheritance.

9. Explanation: This American serial killer shocked the nation when his crimes were revealed. His double life, switching from entertainer to brutal murderer, remains one of the most chilling stories of deception in criminal history.

12. The Ultimate Test: Criminal Challenge

1. Explanation: Luminol is often used to reveal blood traces invisible to the naked eye, as it reacts with the iron in hemoglobin, causing the blood to glow in the dark.

2. Explanation: Fingerprints are unique to each person, making them highly valuable for identifying individuals in criminal cases.

3. Explanation: John Douglas was one of the first FBI agents to begin criminal profiling, creating psychological portraits of criminals that aid in investigations.

4. Explanation: Colin Pitchfork was the first criminal convicted based on DNA analysis in 1988, which confirmed his guilt in the murder of two young girls.

5. Explanation: Blood spatter analysis studies blood patterns to determine details of how injuries occurred and the movement of both the victim and the assailant.

6. Explanation: In cybercrime cases, an IP address is a key piece of evidence, as it can help trace the origin of criminal activities online.

Acknowledgments

Thank you for joining us on this journey through the secrets of criminology! We hope the puzzles, quizzes, and stories in this book brought you both knowledge and enjoyment, sparking your curiosity and inspiring new insights.

Your feedback is incredibly valuable to us. If you have any thoughts, insights, or would like to share your experience with the book, we encourage you to leave a review or reach out to us. Your feedback helps us create even more engaging and informative books for crime enthusiasts like you.

Thank you, and we wish you continued discoveries in the world of mysteries and crime!

www.ingramcontent.com/pod-product-compliance
Lightning Source LLC
LaVergne TN
LVHW012114070526
838202LV00056B/5724